RECKONING WITH MARKETS

RECKONING WITH MARKETS

Moral Reflection in Economics

James Halteman

AND

Edd Noell

OXFORD
UNIVERSITY PRESS

OXFORD
UNIVERSITY PRESS

Oxford University Press, Inc., publishes works that further
Oxford University's objective of excellence
in research, scholarship, and education.

Oxford   New York
Auckland   Cape Town   Dar es Salaam   Hong Kong   Karachi
Kuala Lumpur   Madrid   Melbourne   Mexico City   Nairobi
New Delhi   Shanghai   Taipei   Toronto

With offices in
Argentina   Austria   Brazil   Chile   Czech Republic   France   Greece
Guatemala   Hungary   Italy   Japan   Poland   Portugal   Singapore
South Korea   Switzerland   Thailand   Turkey   Ukraine   Vietnam

Copyright © 2012 by Oxford University Press, Inc.

Published by Oxford University Press, Inc.
198 Madison Avenue, New York, New York 10016
www.oup.com

Oxford is a registered trademark of Oxford University Press

Library of Congress Cataloging-in-Publication Data
Halteman, Jim.
Reckoning with markets : moral reflection in economics /
James Halteman and Edd Noell.
p. cm.
Includes bibliographical references and index.
ISBN 978-0-19-976370-2 (cloth : alk. paper)
1. Economics—Moral and ethical aspects.   I. Noell, Edd S.   II. Title.
HB72.H325 2011
174—dc22
2011014669

1 3 5 7 9 8 6 4 2

Printed in the United States of America
on acid-free paper

*To my wife, Jane, whose work as a spiritual director helps
balance the life of the mind with the life lived. The need
for this balance is an underlying theme in this book.*

J. H.

*To my wife Nancy, servant of the Redeemer. Your loving
encouragement and godly wisdom in innumerable ways
continue to enliven my research and teaching.*

E. N.

CONTENTS

ACKNOWLEDGMENTS

Portions of several chapters, as well as the vignettes located throughout the volume, are the result of a joint project funded by a grant
from the Council for Christian Colleges and Universities (CCCU).
We are grateful for their support in this effort to make the history
of economic thought coupled with moral reflection more relevant
in the undergraduate classroom. We wish also to thank the staff of
Oxford University Press, whose editorial skills made the final draft
a better product.

PREFACE: THE INGREDIENTS
OF A SOCIAL ORDER

This project emerged out of an ongoing dialogue between two economists about the continuing relevance of moral thinking in their discipline. The present volume is intended to encourage both budding and mature economists to engage in a similar discussion. Hopefully such discussions will be enhanced by the exploration of the history of moral reflection in economics presented in the chapters that follow. How we produced the end product involves the story of the pursuit of the elements of social cohesion, a narrative that Jim Halteman most appropriately tells because of his initial interest in probing the distinctive historical elements of 'social glue.'

I was always fascinated by the challenges of maintaining a viable social order. Majoring in history as an undergraduate took me across the span of time and the rise and fall of great civilizations. The flow of intellectual history was a parallel fascination because in each time and place there seemed to be thinkers who tried to dissect the social glue that needed to be nurtured if a given city state, dynasty, or nation was to flourish. Each era had its social and economic institutions coupled with power structures that brought together the various social classes to form a workable existence. And then there were beliefs, values, and religions, acting as oil in the gears of the system. Cultures that could pull together these forces into a complementary package lasted longer than those that tried to survive with contradictory forces at work. For example, a society with centrally controlled political and economic systems will not survive when freedom and social mobility permeate the population or when the tactics used to maintain power become morally offensive.

The moral and ethical components of the social glue may be the most difficult to explore because they are not easily documented and they are often relegated to the level of personal and private contemplation. Organized religion may be the most visible place to study these value-laden forces, but the rhetoric of institutionalized religion does not always match what is really going on in the marketplace or the neighborhood.

My experience nearly two decades ago in Russia and the Czech Republic made this point clear. After Mikhail Gorbachev attempted to open up the Soviet Union to increased Western engagement, I was involved with a group of economists and business faculty who participated in a project to create a curriculum for master of business administration (MBA) programs at some universities in Russia. The minister of education in Russia had committed some resources to add to the funding we had, and the explicit request was to include values into the curriculum along with the market-oriented content. Collecting and translating sources, introducing teachers and students to the material, and adapting it all to reflect Russian culture was a task that involved various visits and stretched out over five years. My group was a wonderful assemblage of Russian academics who cherished the materials we developed and were highly motivated to plough ahead with a values-oriented market-based curriculum. Now, approximately fifteen years after our work concluded, it appears to have failed in its objective.

What went wrong? No doubt there were mistakes made in our strategy and funding. The Ministry of Education was unable to come up with the publishing money. There was resistance to Gorbechev's reform efforts, and on the first day of our first visit in 1991 there was a political coup that attempted to upset Gorbechev's entire program. But a few days later, as I exited the subway to help celebrate the failed coup, I was overwhelmed by the excitement of the crowds that were energized by the possibility of a new future.

As our work progressed, my pessimism began to surface as I realized that there was nothing in markets theory that caused people to trust one another. At one point I asked a Russian professor in the business ethics group whether it would be reflective of Russian culture for a citizen to wake up a sleeping self-service gas station attendant to pay for gas if no one was watching and there was no chance of getting caught for leaving without paying. After a moment of thought, the answer was no. My scenario would be seen as an economic opportunity not a moral issue. This set in motion my search for sources of trust in the culture, and for the most part, I found one main place where trust existed in the early years of independence in the Czech Republic. In a small bolt factory, I watched bolts being made for the European Union by an innovative process developed by the owner and his employees. The owner claimed he could sell much more than he could produce, so I asked him why he did not expand his business. The following conversation gave me some answers to my search for moral glue in the culture:

(OWNER) "I don't have enough cash to build or expand factory facilities."
(ME) "Why not get bank loans and build the plant?"
(OWNER) "I don't trust the banks. They will likely cheat me in the loan process."

(ME) "But couldn't you go to the authorities or police and get justice if the banks did that?

(OWNER) "I don't trust the police either. They are looking out for themselves, not me."

(ME) "Well, who do you trust?"

(OWNER) "I only trust my family, and I have one grandson to take over the business. So getting bigger is not a good plan."

It was becoming clear to me that our efforts to promote markets in the former Soviet Union were going to be a long process with an uncertain outcome no matter how eager many were for change in the system. Without some embedded sense of trust and fair play among the market participants, the cost of transactions was going to be very high. As I left Russia in 1995, one thought kept recurring as I pondered the efforts of the previous five years. How is moral life cultivated in a society, and what makes it grow into something that keeps transaction costs low enough to make market exchanges work?

This study follows the role of philosophers, sages, and religious teachers in the ancient world and moves on to the ruminations on economic justice and influence on everyday economic decisions of the medieval churchmen. With the Reformation comes a new approach to moral reflection and, accompanied by the individualism and scientism of the Enlightenment, moral life is relegated to a more personal and naturalistic, if not emotive, enterprise. Following Adam Smith, telos-based moral reflection and the pursuit of virtue rapidly diminish in economic thought. The market properly constructed is viewed as possessing the necessary ingredients to make moral action wise and profitable. Moral questions can be left to the policy makers who need to make the political and social tradeoffs required for maintaining social solidarity. A common view is that, as recipients of Western religious moral traditions, Western capitalist societies have sufficient moral resources to support market capitalism.

However recent challenges to this view have caused many to wonder if the moral capital of the West is not being rapidly depleted. First, economies are now intertwined worldwide, yet it is hard to foster common values in regard to human rights, environmental responsibility, the rules of exchange, or personal ethics. Second, the complexity of many markets has created an uneven playing field among buyers and sellers increasing the need for individual and corporate integrity if trust is to be maintained. Financial markets and various components of the health care industry are examples of how product complexity makes it difficult for buyers and regulators to play their role in fostering efficient outcomes. The way we think often precedes what we do, and so one objective of this book is to survey the landscape of moral reflection observing how we think about moral life. For generations, economic thinking has carefully maintained a value-free methodology that was designed to predict behavior more than understand it. However, in recent years there has been increased scrutiny of the impact of social norms, customs and habits, psychological predispositions, genetic and neurobiological determinants, and institutional change. This has opened the door to interdisciplinary dialogue and a recognition that moral reflection cannot be ignored as economists seek to both predict behavior and understand the motivation for action.

The story that follows is circuitous and interdisciplinary. It cannot escape philosophical musings, methodological controversies, and historical considerations. Context is all-important, and most interpretations are open to dialogue. As the project progressed, it benefitted from conversations with Professor Edd Noell, a fellow traveler in the history of economic thought literature. His insightful reviews of chapter drafts and his suggestions for additions made it clear that the book would be better if it became a joint project.

Professor Noell's expertise in biblical literature, the medieval period, and Adam Smith and his interest in the heterodox contributions to moral reflection added significantly to the flow of ideas that is important background in understanding how moral and economic life are intertwined. Edd's path on the journey of moral reflection in economic thought has benefited from the light shed by his graduate adviser William Campbell. Bill's nuanced critique of the fact-value distinction and insightful perspective on the moral philosophy of the Scholastics and Adam Smith offer a cogent model of the benefits of rightly understanding economics from the standpoint of the liberal arts.

It is our hope that the following pages will inspire readers to intentionally explore the ways that moral questions impact economic activity and the way they think about how an economy is organized We have aimed particularly to engage undergraduate economics students in the moral dialogue by supplementing their reading in the major primary sources of economic thought with eleven vignettes designed to bring a contemporary application to the historical content of the chapters.

The wall between positive and normative economic thinking is structurally damaged, and this book hopes to consider what repair or changes might be helpful. The hope is that this effort complements and adds value to, rather than competing with, what has been standard practice in economic thinking. As will become clear in chapter 7, the road to economic understanding is never a dead-end street.

RECKONING WITH MARKETS

Chapter 1

Setting the Stage

The Plenary Session

If all of history could be put into one lifetime or one lifetime could stretch across all of history, we could learn so much from the dialogue that might take place among many of the top thinkers of the past. Imagine a conference that would include Aristotle, Saint Paul, Thomas Aquinas, Adam Smith, John Stuart Mill, Jeremy Bentham, Alfred Marshall, Karl Marx, Milton Friedman, Amartya Sen, and many others. Whether the conference is held in Athens, Glasgow, New York, or elsewhere, the crowds would gather to see what kind of discussion would result from the speeches and breakout sessions. Imagine again that the topic for discussion is the role of moral reflection in economic life. What values, beliefs, predispositions, and sentiments are relevant to the allocation of resources in a social order?

Let us do some of the imagining for you; but before we begin, a few caveats are in order. A discussion of moral reflection in economic thinking is different from proposing a specific moral agenda that should be followed. Most of this book is a historical survey of how moral reflection impacted resource allocation over the centuries. Later chapters show how such reflection became suspect in the Enlightenment era of scientific discovery. The latter part of the book considers more recent efforts to expand economic thinking into categories beyond rational choice modeling. Values and beliefs impact preferences, and choices are embedded in data that are often considered value free and are woven into most economic concepts, such as cost and price, and therefore efficiency. The topic of moral reflection in economics raises concerns and fears for many. This is not surprising because differences over moral issues have created enormous conflict and even violence throughout history. Religious fundamentalism, on the one hand, and a passion for autonomy and freedom from restraint, on the other hand, have often ironically led to intolerance and abuse. When people's beliefs become coercive, they frequently are counterproductive. However, in recent times, the moral components embedded in human consciousness have been the subject of increased scrutiny. Interdisciplinary contributions from all the social sciences and humanities are now on the table for discussion and research. Genetics and neurobiology are now integrated into the social sciences and former claims of value-free analysis are being challenged. This book concludes with a discussion of what these developments may mean for economics. It may provide more questions than answers, but hopefully it can encourage more open discussion of how values and beliefs impact economic behavior. So now let our conference on moral reflection in economics begin.

> FACILITATOR: Greetings gentlemen, would you please take your places around the table? The name cards are placed in order of birthdate, and of the various forms of address that have been employed over the centuries, we have chosen to use Mr. when we speak to one another. Our purpose here tonight is to lay out the ground rules for later conversation in the breakout sessions that will follow and to put forward the key issues that need to be addressed at a conference such as this. First, you were invited because you all have made contributions to moral thinking on economic questions.

Some of you have ventured into philosophical and methodological areas, while others have cautioned against making economics a moral science. While we may all see the moral life as an important deterrent to the selfish human passions, we differ on the nature and source of moral reflection. Some understand the source of moral values to lie within the person. Individuals conditioned by social and psychological systems can develop norms and rules that enhance the well-being of the person and the group. Others see moral values as derived from outside the individual, as part of a philosophical or religious belief that presumes a *telos* or ultimate purpose of life. This purpose informs us about the meaning of good and proper conduct of behavior.

Thus we have a common purpose but different approaches, and our task here today is to share our views briefly, not as in a debate but so that those after us in the twenty-first century can see moral reflection as an essential ingredient of economic analysis and policy formation. From this plenary session we will then have breakout sessions in which moral reflection will be explored more deeply through your writings and the work of your contemporaries. The proceedings of the breakout sessions will be summarized and recorded as chapters in a book. And so the floor is open. You may refer to me as the facilitator. Speak into the microphones so that your exact words can be transcribed.

MR. ARISTOTLE, would you like to begin our discussion?

MR. ARISTOTLE: Indeed it would be an honor to do so. "For man, when perfected, is the best of animals, but, when separated from law and justice, he is the worst of all; since armed injustice is the more dangerous, and he is equipped at birth with the arms of intelligence and with moral qualities which he may use for the worst ends. Wherefore, if he have not virtue, he is the most unholy and the most savage of animals, and the most full of lust and gluttony. But justice is the bond of men in states, and the administration of justice, which is the determination of what is just, is the principle of order in political society" (Newman, 7).

FACILITATOR: Mr. Smith, I see your hand first.

MR. SMITH: With all due respect to Mr. Aristotle, it is my belief that "[H]ow selfish soever man may be supposed, there are evidently some principles in his nature, which interest him in the fortune of others, and render their happiness necessary to him though he derives nothing from it except the pleasure of seeing it" (Smith, *TMS*, 1).

FACILITATOR: So it seems as if there is at least some disagreement on the innate nature of people and how that nature is socialized. Does anyone have anything more to say on those topics?

MR. BENTHAM: I must qualify what my esteemed colleagues have said when they relate virtue and some innate selfless instinct as the primary cause of morally good behavior because "[N]ature has placed mankind under the governance of two sovereign masters, pain and pleasure. It is for them alone to point out what we ought to do as well as to determine what we shall do.... They govern us in all we do, in all we say, in all we think: every effort we can make to throw off our subjection, will serve but to demonstrate and confirm it" (Bentham, 166).

FACILITATOR: Mr. Helvetius, you can speak next, but let me emphasize that this discussion is designed to reflect on the role of the moral life in economic activity; so you, as a philosopher, will need to recognize that your audience contains many nonphilosophers.

MR. HELVITIUS: Thank you. Your point is well taken. I simply want to clarify Mr. Bentham's comments because pain and pleasure may be too narrow a framework through which to consider the moral life. Let me suggest that "[A]s the physical world is ruled by the laws of movement so is the moral universe ruled by laws of interest" (Hirschman, 43).

MR. AQUINAS: We seem now to be talking as if we can derive a system whose mechanics will generate moral outcomes. Alleviating pain and pursuing pleasure, or our interests, to use Helvetius's words, certainly is no guarantee that right will prevail in our culture. The following examples illustrate my point that one follows his interest to the detriment of the other. "He who pays usury suffers injustice not from himself but from the usurer, for granted that the usurer does not apply absolute force he nevertheless applies a certain mixed force on him, in that the necessity of having to accept the loan imposes a serious condition so that he returns more than he is given. And it is similar if one reduced to need were to be sold a certain thing for much more than its worth, for that would be an unjust sale just as a usurious loan is unjust" (quoted in Langholm, 1992, 247).

FACILITATOR: OK, does anyone else want to speak to this issue of whether the moral life in a social order is best understood as a corrective of outcomes from the economic system or whether morality is built into the process of the system itself? If the latter is true, will the outcomes be at least as morally defensible as any alternative approach to morality?

MR. MILL, you can be first but let us keep our comments short because it appears many have thoughts on this issue.

MR. MILL: In my view, both approaches have validity. "The laws and conditions of the production of wealth, partake of the character of physical truths. There is nothing optional or arbitrary in them. Whatever mankind produce, must be produced in the modes, and under the condition, imposed by the constitution of external things, and by the inherent properties of their own bodily and mental structure.... It is not so with the Distribution of wealth. That is a matter of human institution solely. The things once there, mankind, individually or collectively, can do with them as they like" (Mill, 349–350).

FACILITATOR: So, in production what is right and good is built into the created system, but in the distribution of things we can alter outcomes to achieve justice. Does anyone what to challenge that idea?

MR. FRIEDMAN: I disagree with Mr. Mill's division of production and distribution into mechanical and moral parts. The market has clear principles of both production and distribution. When we view economics as science, I'll call that positive economics, we are only attempting to predict what outcomes will follow. Because our positive science is not perfect, we sometimes come up with different predictions that lead to disagreements. I believe that "[L]aymen and experts alike are inevitably tempted to shape positive conclusions to fit strongly held normative preconceptions and to reject positive conclusions if their normative implications—or what are said to be their normative implications—are unpalatable. Positive economics is in principle independent of any particular ethical position or normative judgments.... In short, positive economics is, or can be, an 'objective' science in precisely the same sense as any of the physical sciences.... I venture the judgment that currently in the Western world and especially in the United States, differences about economic policy among disinterested citizens derive predominantly from different predictions about the economic consequences of taking action—differences that in principle can be eliminated by progress of positive economics—rather than from fundamental differences about which men can ultimately only fight" (Friedman, 4–5).

MR. MARX: Mr. Friedman uses this positive/normative dichotomy to build a system that isolates moral reflection from the methods of economic analysis. Yet a system built on individual fulfillment of desire using competition as the driving force cannot ignore the moral implications of its practices. "The bourgeoisie, wherever it has got the upper hand, has put an end to all feudal, patriarchal, idyllic relations. It has pitilessly torn asunder the motley feudal ties that bound man to his 'natural superiors,' and has left remaining no other nexus between man and man than naked self-interest, that callous 'cash payment.' It has drowned the most heavenly ecstasies of religious fervor, of chivalrous enthusiasm, of philistine sentimentalism, in the icy water of egotistical calculation. It has resolved personal worth into exchange value, and in place of the numberless indefeasible chartered freedoms, has set up that single, unconscionable freedom— Free Trade. In a word, for exploitation, veiled by religious and political illusions, it has substituted naked, shameless, direct, brutal exploitation" (Marx, TCM, 91–92).

MR. MARSHALL: In my opinion, Mr. Marx goes overboard in his critique of a market system. However, "[T]here are two great questions which we cannot think too much about. The first is, Is it necessary that, while there is so much wealth, there should be so much want? The second is, Is there not a great fund of conscientiousness and unselfishness latent to the breasts of men, both rich and poor which could be called out if the problems of life were set before them in the right way, and which would cause misery and poverty rapidly to diminish?" (Pigou, 83).

MR. MILL: Mr. Marshall makes a good point. "But if public spirit, generous sentiments, or true justice and equality are desired, association, not isolation, of interests, is the school in which these excellences are nurtured. The aim of improvement should be not solely to place human beings in a condition in which they will be able to do without one another, but to enable them to work with or for one another in relations not involving dependence" (Mill, 128).

MR. SAY: Perhaps there is a way to bring together this public spirit with the pursuit of self-interest. "That each individual is interested in the general prosperity of all, and that the success of one branch of industry promotes that of all the others. In fact whatever profession or line of business a man may devote himself to, he is the better paid and the more readily finds employment, in proportion as he sees others thriving equally around him" (Say, 1824).

FACILITATOR: Mr. Walras, do you have something to add to this effort to link production, distribution, and moral reflection?

MR. WALRAS: Yes, "[T]hough our description of free competition emphasizes the problem of utility, it leaves the question of justice entirely to one side, since our sole object has been to show how a certain distribution of services gives rise to a certain distribution of products. The question of the (original) distribution of services remains open however" (Walras, 262).

FACILITATOR: What I hear you saying is that if we redistributed resources of production first, the market system could then function effectively and justly. In this way, you see moral questions separated from the workings of the market. Does anyone want to add to this?

MR. KEYNES: We clearly need a balance of market efficiency and social oversight. "For my part, I think that Capitalism, wisely managed, can probably be made more efficient for attaining economic ends than any alternative system yet in sight, but that in itself it is in many ways extremely objectionable. Our problem is to work out a social organization which shall be as efficient as possible without offending our notions of a satisfactory way of life" (Keynes 2003, 595).

MR. BENTHAM: I remain skeptical of this blending of private and public interest to achieve some moral and efficient outcome. "The interest of the community is one of the most general expressions that can occur in the phraseology of morals: no wonder that the meaning of it is often lost. When it has a meaning it is this. The community is a fictitious body, composed of the individual persons who are considered as constituting as it were its members. The interest of the community then is what?—the sum of the interest of the several members who compose it" (Bentham 1954, 166).

MR. SMITH: What seems to be missing in much of this conversation is some appeal to what is instilled by nature in not only economic relationships but also in us as individuals. We are not simply free to choose from the list of virtues what we will do. We are, in fact, highly interdependent. Perhaps we can abstain from benevolence without rebuke but "[T]here is, however, another virtue, of which the observance is not left to the freedom of our own wills, which may be extorted by force, and of which the violation exposes to resentment, and consequently to punishment. This virtue is justice: the violation of justice is injury: it does real and positive hurt to some particular persons from motives which are naturally disapproved of. It is, therefore the proper object of resentment, and of punishment which is the natural consequence of resentment" (Smith, TMS, 79). I might add that these sentiments that we share with our peers are not just social norms. Rather "[T]he all wise Author of Nature has, in this manner, taught man to respect the sentiments and judgments of his brethren; to be more or less pleased when they approve of his conduct, and to be more or less hurt when they disapprove of it. He has made man, if I may say so, the immediate judge of mankind; and has, in this respect, as in many others, created him after his own image, and appointed him his vicegerent upon earth, to superintend the behaviour of his brethren" (Smith, TMS, 128–130).

MR. VEBLEN: While I agree that moral life in economic affairs involves interdependence among people, I would argue that moral conduct does not result from natural behavior that is instilled by a creator, as Mr. Smith implies. Instead "[s]ocial evolution is a process of selective adaptation of temperament and habits of thought under the stress of the circumstances of associated life. The adaptation of habits of thought is the growth of institutions. But along with the growth of institutions has gone a change of a more substantial character. Not only have the habits of men changed with the changing exigencies of the situation, but these changing exigencies have brought about a correlative change in human nature" (Veblen, 1983, 213).

MR. HAYEK: We need to be careful to focus on broad general principles of moral conduct rather than on specific behaviors or detailed definitions of justice. "In the small group the individual can know the effects of his actions on his several fellows, and the rules may effectively forbid him to harm them in any manner and even require him to assist them in specific ways. In the Great Society many of the effects of a person's actions on various fellows must be unknown to him. It can, therefore, not be the specific effects in the particular case, but only rules which define kinds of actions prohibited or required, which must serve as guides to the individual" (Hayek, 1976, 90). While Mr. Veblen and I disagree often on the point of the evolution of social norms and principles, we have some common ground. Mr. Smith may be pushing it too far when he claims that a God force external to people brings in an outside purpose or telos into human nature. It is not easy to make that idea operational.

MR. SEN: In many ways I think we have much in common here as we seek to explore how the moral life and economic analysis are interrelated in our work. I prefer to use the word engineering rather than mechanical when we speak of positive methodology, but "[G]iven the nature of economics, it is not surprising that both the ethics-related origin and the engineering-based origin of economics have some cogency of their own. I would like to argue that the deep questions raised by the ethics-related view of motivation and of social achievement must find an important place in modern economics, but at the same time it is impossible to deny that the engineering approach has much to offer to economics as well" (Sen, 6).

FACILITATOR: We have covered a great deal of ground in this plenary session, and all those who contributed have helped to define the issues that need to be addressed in the breakout sessions that will be structured according to various periods in history. Clearly we did not have time to have everyone offer the full context of his comments, but the issues raised can be fleshed out in the sessions to follow. Hopefully many more of you will be able to contribute in those sessions.

As is apparent from the discussion so far, moral reflection in economic life was deeply embedded in thought and practice up until at least the sixteenth century. After Adam Smith, late-eighteenth-century economic thinking became the science of economics, and moral questions were viewed as nonscientific and so less relevant to analytical economic studies. The sessions that follow examine the historical trends from the ancient world to the present time, concluding with some speculation as to where moral reflection is headed in the years ahead.

There are several guidelines we need to follow as we move into our breakout sessions. First, because we come from so many different social and historical contexts, it is important to understand one another in light of the historical situation from which a comment is made. Second, because we are hoping to shed light on economic concerns of modern times, we need to use language that speaks to those working in economics who may not have significant training in philosophy, ethics, religion, or any of the other relevant disciplines. In the modern era, the specialization of academic life has made truly integrative thinking difficult. Third, let us recognize that the complexity of moral life in economics makes conclusive answers elusive. Our job is to pose the relevant questions and offer our relevant insights in the hope of stimulating ongoing fruitful dialogue about the nature of moral reflection in economic studies.

What we have been calling breakout sessions will now be referred to as chapters. In chapter 2 the Greek, Hebrew, and Stoic understandings of economic moral life are explored. Why is the moral life important? Do moral claims come from within us and our ability to construct a meaningful ethical system, or is a moral purpose being served beyond our own social interactions? Chapter 3 examines the way moral reflection in economic matters was understood by Christian thinkers in the medieval period. Appropriate resource allocation required a discernment of what was just, in general, and how resources should be distributed, in particular. Religion and social administration became linked, and God became the source of moral reflection. Chapter 4 tells the story of how the Enlightenment revolutionized the foundations of all that went before it. Key to this movement was the work of Adam Smith and others who related the moral life to our built-in passions and instincts while holding at arms length any external source informing our sense of right and wrong. While it was not Smith's purpose to secularize social analysis, later classical economists, discussed in chapter 5, moved increasingly to a mechanical scientific model of economic behavior. Chapter 6 looks at several heterodox figures who in varied ways either challenged the new approach or refused to adopt it without significant qualification. Chapter 7 considers the resulting methodology of Enlightenment economics and how the positive-normative divide moved moral reflection entirely outside the bounds of economic analysis. Chapter 8 looks forward to the impact of many contemporaries who go beyond the rational choice boundaries into social norms, values and beliefs, psychological predispositions, theories of cooperation, cultural conditioning, and the biochemistry of the mind. Many of these frontiers open the door to renewed moral reflection and its impact on behavior. Finally chapter 9 sketches out a simple framework meant to foster a broader, more interdisciplinary approach to economic thinking and the moral life. At the end of each chapter are short vignettes that relate the concepts discussed in the chapter to contemporary issues.

These chapters will not be exhaustive treatments of each topic. Rather they are intended to foster discussion and further efforts to fill in the gaps that are left by each presentation. If social interaction is enhanced by moral commitments and if personal well-being is realized more fully in the exercise of moral virtue, then economists would do well to enrich their work with moral input, as Adam Smith did so well. While the conference conveners (the authors) are motivated in this work by their commitment to the Christian religion, anyone who believes the moral life is an essential part of the social glue is a fellow traveler in this venture. All have something valuable to contribute to the discussion.

Chapter 2

Moral Reflection in the Ancient Mediterranean World

Most contemporary economists pay little attention to the ancient world and the thinkers that it produced. There are at least four related reasons for this oversight that must be understood before the Greek philosophers and other writers of premodern days will be accepted as part of the framework of a trained economist.

First, the population was largely illiterate, and there was a notion that some people were inherently better prepared to lead or rule others. This led to a stratified social order in which the few thought for the many and slaves were viewed as necessary in the social system. Life for the members of the lower class was dismal at best. To highly literate societies with democratic traditions and social mobility, the ideal state of Plato and the social stratification of Plato, Aristotle, Saint Paul, and the Roman world seem offensive if not immoral.

Second, the ancient world was largely devoid of what we would call technology. While Aristotle's notion of specialization of labor was similar to Adam Smith's view on the topic, except that Aristotle thought people were born with specialties and Smith viewed the differences as learned, Aristotle's world did not have the technological support to make the concept of universal opulence thinkable. Consequently, for the masses, bare subsistence was the expectation and for the elite thinkers a simple life was also considered appropriate. Royalty, on the other hand, lived sumptuously off the surplus of slave labor. New technology would have added little to the lifestyle of the rulers and, in the hands of potentially rebellious slaves, might have been used against the elites. Contemporary social analysts, who are inclined to see history as a cumulative process of progress and technological advance, often see earlier periods in history as inferior and as having little to offer the present.

Third, the philosophers of the ancient world highlighted the notion of human telos, which led to concerns about equity and justice. For Plato, Aristotle, Augustine, Thomas Aquinas, and even the Stoic thinkers, moral precepts reflected the notion of telos that was preordained by some creator force or transcendent being. Telos involved some concept of what people were meant to be. People lived in a constant dialogue between human nature and the ultimate purpose of their existence. Out of that dialogue came the moral precepts, or ethics, that ordered life. Because of these beliefs, the early philosophers and scholarly writers up through the Middle Ages considered issues of purpose and meaning the most pressing questions in economic life. Were resources handled in a just and fair manner, given the constraints, and was the entire community meaningfully sustained? Behavior was measured in terms of right and good rather than by how free people were to express their individual preferences or how much output could be generated. Production was thought to be generally stable at the subsistence level and only partially under human control. Economics, if it had existed as a discipline, would have been concerned that everyone had his or her fair share of output determined largely by need and station in life. Growth rather than survival has become the key challenge today, and efficiency and output, rather than moral dialogue, are the metric of what is right and good.

The fourth reason why most people today ignore premodern thinkers stems from the first three reasons. Because social stratification was thought to be necessary, because a subsistence level of income for the masses was the norm, and because the thinking elite considered moral reflection to be essential, it seemed natural that survival could be achieved best in the context of the group. Instead of the classical economists' attempts to create an order that would promote universal opulence for the population, Aristotle and Plato thought more in terms of human flourishing within the community, or polis, despite material limitations. The group superseded the individual in ancient thought, whereas the opposite is true in modern economics.

Despite these biases against ancient thinkers and notwithstanding the miserable conditions the masses of the ancient world endured, it is appropriate to begin a discussion of moral reflection in economics with the thinkers who are at the foundation of our Western intellectual heritage. One needs to be clear about the concept of moral virtue when reading Plato and Aristotle. While they certainly are dealing in the categories that modern economists would call normative economics and while their view of what is real included a reality beyond what is commonly perceived, the use of the term *moral virtue* did not have religious overtones. One of the reasons why philosophical inquiry flourished among the Greeks is because of their view that the gods were not particularly invested in the natural world. The fact that the search for truth was not bound by religious assumptions opened the door to a full inquiry of the telos of life and a debate about how that purpose might be lived out. There was no national religion in Greece at the time. This lack of religious fervor in Greek thought means that Aristotle's view of moral virtue must be clarified so as not to appear to be more than he intended it to be.

It is also important to recognize the difficulties of historical analysis when the context of earlier times is significantly different from the present. Unlike the staged dialogue that opened this book, we do not have the benefit of listening to Aristotle or Epictetus debate with Adam Smith on the concept of natural law or the specialization of labor. Nor can we observe a debate between Thomas Aquinas and Milton Friedman on the nature of freedom and value-free economics. Ancient texts interpreted through a modern lens can frequently lead to misreadings.

Despite these difficulties, this book follows the flow of the intellectual process in economics observing moral reflection wane from its place of active dialogue. Hopefully, readers will be left with enough questions to stimulate ongoing exploration and enough answers to make one suspicious of value-free economics, which is more often preached than practiced in our time.

As is the case in any social analysis, the starting point is the nature of the actors in the system and the nature of the system in which they function. For Aristotle, people were seen as part of a larger whole, that is, the polis or state. The state is not formed to serve the individual by regulating producers, forming cooperative arrangements among consumers or ensuring property rights. Rather, the state exists so that a person can become whole, and as such, it is prior to the individual or the family. "The proof that the state is a creation of nature and prior to the individual is that the individual, when isolated, is not self-sufficing" (Aristotle, 7). This is the first building block in Aristotle's morally virtuous society. Without the state, the person quickly degenerates into a lawless unjust creature. Speaking of the condition of humanity, Aristotle claims of that individual that "if he have not virtue, he is the most unholy and the most savage of animals, and the most full of lust and gluttony" (Aristotle, 7). Fortunately with the application of properly constructed concepts of virtue and the state, people can become the highest order beings.

This transformative process begins with the capacity or potential that Aristotle called *dynamis.* Being human gives people an inner inertia to realize the purpose for which they were created. From birth people move from the potential to the actual, a process that Aristotle called *entelicheia*. For humans the movement to actuality involves a striving for the greatest good through the use of reason and contemplation. While the creative force draws all things toward perfection, the process is not without obstacles to which the individual and the state must pay careful attention.

But what is the greatest good of humanity, and how does one achieve that end without giving in to corrupt practices? There is a short answer and a long explanation that can be used in discussing this question. The short answer is that the goal is happiness and morally virtuous behavior is the means. Unfortunately, both parts of this answer involve translations from the Greek to English that are inadequate at best and misleading at worst.

Perhaps considering what happiness is not will help in conveying Aristotle's meaning of happiness. First, it is not simply what brings an individual a good feeling or pleasing experience, though those sensations are not excluded from happiness. Second, happiness is not something that exists in a moment of time but is rather a state of being about which one may be conscious or unconscious at any given time. Third, happiness cannot be attained by fulfilling acquired wishes or preferences. It comes only when our natural desires and needs are fulfilled. Fourth, happiness is not unique to each individual because it is derived from universal principles that prescribe what is genuinely good for us. Thus, to understand Aristotle's happiness concept we need to move beyond the individualistic notion that each person has a unique preference function that, when optimized, results in the maximum amount of happiness possible. We need to find those practices that lead to true happiness and a flourishing life. People today tend to connect happiness, material plenty, and pleasure, while Aristotle had a much deeper view of happiness. Unfortunately, his Greek word *eudemonia*, commonly rendered as "happiness" implies to us a feeling of pleasure rather than a vision of what is truly a flourishing life.

Because there is consistency to creation and because we are designed to fit into the natural patterns of the created order, it follows that genuine happiness and the good life will consist of similar ingredients for everyone. Accordingly, it is the task of a social order to uncover what contributes to the good life and then to educate people to exercise practices that promote that life. The philosopher's responsibility is to search out what is truly good for people and to then construct a polis that can foster that good life and therefore true happiness. In his philosophical role, Aristotle identifies the obvious external goods that are needed to create and support the good life. Food, shelter, clothing, and some degree of freedom are essential to the good life. Positive attributes and internal qualities such as friendship, honor, and self esteem are also necessary for happiness, but moderation and good intentions are important qualifiers of all the elements and influences that provide people with a genuinely happy life. Alasdair Macintyre defines eudemonia as "the state of being well and doing well in being well, of a man's being well-favored himself and in relation to the divine" (MacIntyre 148).

If the goal is true happiness, what is the preferred means to the goal? Aristotle's answer is moral virtue but, as with happiness, the term needs some fleshing out. Due to the tendency of people who are outside or on the fringes of the polis to pursue what is not good for them, there needs to be boundaries, social norms, an articulated group vision, and models of how people should act in order to achieve the good life. Virtue results from one's ability to embrace and integrate the internal and external requirements for happiness despite the temptation to do otherwise. It could be translated excellence, as in an athletic contest when someone performs a perfect routine. The athletic metaphor is actually helpful in understanding

virtue. When one forgoes all the easy alternative activities of pleasure and trains vigorously to achieve what becomes a perfect performance, one is considered virtuous.

What results in the process is a body that responds automatically
in many ways because the training has made many of the necessary
moves habitual. The athlete wins because he has made himself athletic, and it is out of that athleticism that the desired results follow.
The same is true in life if one commits to the goal of happiness and
diligently practices the internal and external aspects of happiness,
then that person is developing virtue. When the practice leads to a
way of life that is habitual, we can say that the person is virtuous.
You become what you intentionally practice.

Unfortunately, virtuous people are rare and almost nonexistent
unless the polis or social order is structured in such a way that virtue
is fostered. Laws must be fashioned promoting right behavior, and
those most inclined to discern and practice virtue are to be leaders of
the state. The philosopher should be king, and people need to learn
their place in the social structure. This vision was not designed to
set up a benevolent dictator but to develop a polis that could thrive,
given the variety of people, their social status, and their differences
in education levels. Certainly a philosopher king who did not function out of moral virtue could bring down the entire system.

At this point it is important to consider more carefully the concept of the moral in the term *moral virtue*. In modern literature, the
term *moral* comes into play when dialogue about right and wrong is
necessary before one can proceed. If one takes enough food to live
reasonably well, that may be virtuous behavior since to do otherwise would lead to death, which certainly is not an element of happiness and the good life. Yet there is no moral dialogue required
in discerning whether such behavior is appropriate. On the other
hand, when choices between alternative and worthy courses of
action need to be made, when immediate versus future welfare is

involved, when questions of what is enough need to be posed, and when tradeoffs between ourselves and others present themselves then a dialogue about right and wrong cannot be avoided.

In Aristotle's scheme of things, such dialogical moral reflection is essential to the structuring of a social order. When people love one another, as in a healthy family, such reflection will result in morally virtuous behavior, which in turn leads to happiness. However, in the larger polis, moral reflection will likely not compel the moral behavior necessary to provide a flourishing life for the masses unless the reflection leads to laws and rules that are institutionalized. Aristotle calls this justice, and he sees justice as being as important to happiness as the acts of virtue are: "Justice is the bond of men in states, and the administration of justice, which is the determination of what is just, is the principle of order in political society" (Aristotle, 7). Both justice and virtue are required for happiness, and both require moral dialogue in order to be fully operative. This implies that social organization is both natural and purposeful. It is natural in that it is necessary to serve a need that is natural in creation. It is purposeful in that the form of organization is left to humans to design. As Mortimer J. Adler has suggested,

> In Aristotle's view, families, tribes, and states are no more the products of instinct than are schools, clubs, and business organizations. They are not like bees and ant mounds, which for a given species of bee or ant are always organized in exactly the same way, generation after generation, and wherever you find particular species of bee or ant. But though all human beings belong to the same species, we find quite different patterns of association and organization in human families, tribes, and states. That, according to Aristotle, indicates that these societies were, in origin, voluntarily and purposefully formed, and

formed with some plan of organization that the human beings
involved thought up for themselves.

(Adler, 111)

Such a thought process requires considerable moral dialogue,
and so the formation of a social order, in Aristotle's view, is far from
a natural process that is devoid of moral judgment. This is some
distance from Friedrich Hayek's modern view that social organization is ideally a natural, spontaneous process that is not formed by
people and is not subject to human adjustments from a process of
moral dialogue. Moral reflection is central to the way Aristotle and
the Greek philosophers viewed their work in regard to economic
life and all other aspects of the social order.

It must be emphasized that, to Aristotle, moral reasoning did
not imply some input from the gods, though it did suggest a right
relationship with the divine. The purpose of moral reflection was
to achieve happiness and the good life of virtue, but that purpose
constituted a powerful telos for Aristotle. It is also important to
keep in mind that, unlike modern market theory, the good life was
not some socially efficient ideal derived from individual preferences
that get expressed in an impersonal market.

Given this notion of happiness as a goal and of moral virtue as a
means of achieving that telos, it is instructive to see how this worked
itself out in economic relationships. Both Aristotle and Plato see the
impact of the division of labor in economic life. In Plato's *Republic*
there is a discussion showing how specialization enhances output
and leads to increased trade. As the standard of living rises, the bor-
ders of the state are confining, and so expansion is necessary and
results in war. In Plato's words, "[n]ow we have discovered war to
be derived from causes which are also the causes of almost all the
evils in States, private as well as public" (Plato 66). Thus prosperity

and the human desire for luxury subvert the goal of happiness in Plato's ideal state. The solution to the economic problem of scarcity is to desire less by having people realize the virtue of a simple life. Most Greek thinkers, the Hebrews of the Old Testament times, and the Christian church throughout the Middle Ages all focused primarily on this problem of human desires rather than on the production side of the economic problem. The production process and its resulting rewards were considered to be governed more by nature than human ingenuity.

Aristotle, after recognizing the primacy of the state, focused more on the household as the economic unit for analysis:

> Seeing then that the state is made up of households, before speaking of the state we must speak of the management of the household.... Now we should begin by examining everything in its least elements; and the first and least parts of a family are master and slave, husband and wife, father and children. We have therefore to consider what each of these three relations is and ought to be.
>
> (Aristotle, 7)

In Aristotle's search for what is and ought to be in economic life, the notion of what was natural was the guiding principle. Aristotle defined natural as follows: "For what each thing is when fully developed, we call its nature, whether speaking of a man, a horse, or a family. Besides, the final cause and end of a thing is the best, and to be self-sufficing is the end and the best" (Aristotle, 6).

Aristotle's economic analysis promotes a life well lived by trying to uncover the final cause or the nature of an entity beginning with the household. In nearly all matters there are natural and unnatural aspects. A shoe's purpose is for walking rather than to be an object of speculation for monetary gain. Accordingly, the former use is natural and right, while the second use is unnatural and wrong. Exchanging shoes for their use is an appropriate reason for trade, and money as a medium of exchange is natural for that purpose.

Aristotle's evaluation of trade should be understood in the context of ancient Mediterranean economies. Whether it is the setting of the Greek polis, pharaoh's Egypt, or Israel's tribes ruled by a monarch, the gains from the division of labor are allocated by several means: redistribution, reciprocity, and commercial trade. In the first case, the state collects products for redistribution (as when a Greek king might gather the bounty secured from a war and determine how it is to be distributed) or decides to divide honors among its citizenry. Aristotle declares that this kind of activity must be governed by distributive justice. This requires that account be taken of the proper proportion each should receive based on the position of the recipients. Reciprocity, as equal exchange, involves the exchange of products on a small scale among families or neighbors in a village without the maximization of gain as the primary motivation. These people are of similar social standing and means, and so equal exchanges are just. It often consists of ritualized gift giving. However as society grows and exchanges occur among individuals of different stations in life, reciprocity as an equal exchange must be altered to consider proportionate benefits. Aristotle is clear that proportionality relates to need. If I make shoes and want to buy food from a farmer, proportionate justice would mean that after the exchange, we would have derived the same value from each commodity exchanged. In modern terms, if my marginal utility for food was very high and if my trading partner's marginal utility for shoes was relatively low, then I would get more food per pair of shoes than if the beginning utilities were reversed. In Aristotle's words, "Reciprocity will be secured, then, when things are equalized, so that the shoemaker's product is to the farmer's as the farmer is to the shoemaker. However, they must be introduced into the figure of proportion not when they have already exchanged and one extreme has both excesses, but when they still have their own; in that way they will be equals and associates, because this sort of equality can be found in them" (Aristotle, 130). In other words, the exchange rate must be based on the difference in the marginal utilities before exchange or there would be no incentive to trade.

With the growth of the polis through the division of labor, Plato, Aristotle, and other Greek thinkers acknowledge the need for commercial trade relying on a monetary medium. However, for Aristotle, retail trade is problematic when it involves gains for a middleman who is viewed as producing nothing. Such exchanges foster greed and excess. "Hence we may infer that retail trade is not a natural part of the art of money-making; had it been so, men would have ceased to exchange when they had enough" (Aristotle, 8) Aristotle finally summarizes his case against chrematistics (his designation of the unnatural use of money) as follows: "Thus then, we have considered the art of money-making, which is unnecessary, and why men want it; and also the necessary art of money-making, which we have seen to be different from the other, and to be a natural part of the art of managing a household, concerned with the provision of food, not, however, like the former kind, unlimited, but having a limit" (Aristotle, 10). Thus Aristotle evaluates all forms of economic exchange in light of their place in promoting virtue and in serving the telos of household economic activity.

The purpose of this discussion is not to exhaust Aristotle's views on economic matters but to illustrate the manner in which Greek thinkers approached economic issues. Four things stand out:

1. The economic problem of scarcity can best be handled by limiting wants rather than increasing production. Happiness and the life well lived were not found in the fulfillment of unlimited wants.

2. There is a difference between wants and needs, and this difference can be understood when we realize our true nature and our true purpose in life (our telos).

3. Understanding our true nature requires considerable moral reflection and the cultivation of moral virtues. It is important to realize that what is natural to Aristotle does not refer to the order of a mechanistic world system. Rather, what is natural is what contributes to the final cause or purpose of existence. What truly leads to happiness and a life well lived is natural even if humans tend toward behavior that detracts from true happiness. What is natural is what is truly good for us, and that will be consistent with our human telos.

4. Any considerations of final causes or moral virtues were undertaken from the context of the group (body politic) rather than from the orientation of individual preference patterns, and so proportionality and equality are important values to maintain.

While it is possible to view ancient philosophy as supportive of a highly stratified and largely subsistent social order it is also true that the simple life was practiced by these thinkers and, as in the case of Socrates, virtue was practiced even when it led to premature death. The acceptance of a type of slavery and male dominance in ancient times was due to the view that these ideologies were necessary for the social order to survive. The Greek thinkers, however, sought to make those institutions as benign as possible, and thus concerns about economic justice assumed an egalitarian tone.

While Aristotle and Plato dominated the ancient philosophical scene and have been key influences ever since, it is appropriate to consider the views of Hesiod as well for the contrasting perspective he offers. Barry Gordon sees Hesiod as relating more to the free farmers and slaves of the ancient world. Hesiod claims that "men never rest from labour and sorrow by day and from perishing by night" (Gordon 3). For Hesiod the life well lived and happiness were dreams beyond reach of the average person because "the gods keep hidden from men the means of life" (Gordon 3). People work to eke out an existence, to avoid social shame, and to keep up with their peers in the social order. Striving and competition are means to these simple goals. In other words, Hesiod focused more on increasing production to meet basic needs. This attention to increasing production in a world of scarcity seems considerably removed from Aristotle's focus on the goal of happiness and moral virtue in an environment of sufficiency. In every age there is some distance between the concerns of the masses that focus on simple production and the contemplations of the thinkers who sometimes see happiness and material accumulation as unrelated.

In later chapters, the case will be made that economics has emphasized means and largely ignored ends despite the fact that questions of purpose are connected to human welfare. The claim here is that the discipline ignores each particular emphasis at its peril. Figure 2.1 summarizes the predominant Greek philosophical position as articulated in Aristotle's ethical theory. We must be in constant dialogue with the gap between our human nature and our purpose for existence if we are to thrive as a civilization. The exercise of moral reflection and the practice of ethical norms are the means by which our nature and our telos are mediated.

While the Greek philosophers represent a nonreligious approach to moral reflection where the telos is not cast in transcendent terms, there are other influential streams of thought paralleling the Greeks that were decidedly religious and transcendent in their approach.

Centuries before the Greeks but with minimal influence at the time, the Hebrews of the Palestine area developed a monotheistic worldview that has become the core of theology for at least two

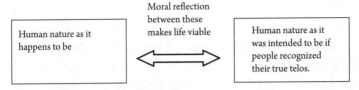

Figure 2.1 The Context of Moral Reflection

major religious groups today. Both Jews and Christians look to the Old Testament as an authoritative source of religious beliefs, and Christians see the New Testament as a sacred text as well. In these core sacred texts, moral reflection is the lens through which all behavior is conditioned. The Hebrew God, Yahweh, spoke directly through Moses and the prophets articulating the law from which behavioral norms were established. The Old Testament affirms that humans are distinctive among all of creation for being made in God's image. Yahweh calls them to serve Him through loving others as themselves (Leviticus 19:18). At the same time, the Old Testament describes the fall of humanity into sinfulness due to a rebellion against God. The Hebrew view of human nature involves a concept of human depravity that, apart from redemption by God, is destructive to social organization and human well-being. Similarly, Aristotle is not optimistic about human nature (except that when properly conditioned it can be socially constructive); however his lack of sanguinity about human character does not stem from any conception of sin against a holy God and His revealed word.

The Hebrew Bible portrays social life as organized around the tribes of Israel. For them, the tribal social structure of ancient Israel is similar to the Greek polis except that Yahweh, rather than the philosophers, was the guiding influence. Yahweh's qualities of love and justice were expressed through detailed law and practiced, when the people were faithful, in a carefully structured community life. The fortunes of the Hebrew nation rose and fell according to their obedience to the law and Yahweh's commands. Moreover, the Old Testament depicts how Israel's social life was to be structured so that the evil aspects of human nature might be directed in a redemptive fashion (Halteman 1995). The Hebrew Scriptures affirm that, in following Yahweh's wisdom, Israel would be a redemptive light to the nations (Deuteronomy 4:5–6).

A significant portion of Yahweh's law for Israel addresses economic life among the tribes in ancient Palestine. It is concerned positively with the provision of sustenance through the tribes and, within them, the individual families. Kinship relationships involving reciprocity played a significant role in shaping exchange in Israel's agrarian economy. Thus, for example, a follower of Yahweh is expected to not only produce for his immediate family but also fulfill his duty with respect to his covenantal obligations to others in terms of the agricultural harvest. When one landholder obtains a surplus, reciprocity requires that he share produce with his kin or neighbor who experiences a poor crop (Schaefer and Noell). However, exchange motivated by economic gain frequently occurs. The Hebrew Bible addresses the nature of justice in commercial trade. It is most specific about injustice in exchange, for it prohibits deceit, fraud, and coercion. In ancient Israel it was easy for deceitful traders to cheat the poor, widow, orphan, or sojourner. These groups had little or no claim to the land as a key economic resource, so they had the fewest economic options. To enforce what the Old Testament prophets term their "rights" not to be oppressed in the marketplace, the landless disadvantaged turn to the elders at the gate to receive gleaning rights from the field as a means of sustenance. The elders (and eventually the king) require traders to perform their essential duty of fair dealing (Noell 2007b).

The New Testament is full of teachings relating to how believers should treat the poor and wealthy, what is involved in the responsible stewardship of resources, and how true spiritual well-being can be corrupted by economic concerns. In the Sermon on the Mount in the New Testament Gospels, Jesus declares what is a constant theme among early Christians:

> No one can serve two masters, for either he will hate the one and love the other, or he will be devoted to the one and despise the other. You cannot serve God and money. Therefore I tell you, do not anxious about your life, what you will eat or what you will drink, nor about your body, what you will put on. Is not life more than food, and the body more than clothing? Look at the birds of the air: they neither sow nor reap nor gather into barns, and yet your heavenly Father feeds them. Are you not of more value than they?
>
> (Matthew 6:24–26)

As in the Old Testament, the New Testament gospels include teaching on justice in transactions (Noell 2007a). The Gospel writers note practices of economic injustice by tax collectors and Roman soldiers (Luke 3:12–14). Jesus's encounters with the tax collector Zacchaeus (Luke 19:1–10) and cleansing of the Temple by driving out the money changers (Mark 11:15–17) both speak to injustice in exchange. The New Testament letters take up the same theme. For example, we read that the laborer is worthy of his wage (I Timothy 5:18). Applying this principle, the apostle James declares to the rich landowner that he is robbing his farm laborers by not paying them: "Behold, the wages of the laborers who mowed your fields, which you kept back by fraud, are crying out against you, and the cries of the harvesters have reached the ears of the Lord of hosts" (James 5:4). The apostle Paul says that employers are to give their workers justice (Colossians 4:1). While no specific just wage is identified in the New Testament, the stress is on the employer's obligation before God to treat his laborers fairly. These examples emphasize that, for the Christian, it is hard to escape the idea that all behavior including economic concerns is subject to moral reflection.

By the time of the Greek philosophers, the glory days of the Hebrew nation were over, but the worldview of a transcendent God who deeply cared about creation and His people had hardly taken hold. In the Christian tradition, God becomes incarnate in Jesus of Nazareth, who communicates the essence of true human telos and what moral precepts are needed to live in harmony with the telos of life. The basis for moral reflection in the Christian world can be seen in the words of Jesus from Matthew 22:37–40: "And he said to him, 'You shall love the Lord your God with all your heart and with all your soul and with all your mind. This is the great and first commandment. And a second is like it: You shall love your neighbor as yourself. On these two commandments depend all the Law and the Prophets.'" A considerable portion of the biblical teaching critiques the heavily stratified nature of the ancient social order yet doesn't call for social upheaval. Thus, in Paul's command to Onessimus, slave owners are taught to treat their slaves well rather than to free them outright. Concurrent with both the Greek and Hebrew writings is another group of thinkers who have had less influence over time but who caught the attention of Adam Smith in the eighteenth century; so their contribution is noteworthy. Stoic philosophy, first established by Zeno in 300 BCE, was kept alive by a series of philosophers for more than five hundred years. Though many of the original works from this group have been lost, the thinking of philosophers such as Cicero, Seneca, Epictetus, and Marcus Aurelius stand out because they were complementary to concepts that surfaced again in the Enlightenment. Three issues will be highlighted here as significant background to moral reflection on economic matters.

When Adam Smith examines the role of nature in moral philosophy, when he considers the quality of self-control in human behavior, and when he addresses the happy and contented life, he frequently enters into dialogue with Stoic positions on these issues. Stoics were materialists in that they saw the created order as the reference point for understanding human existence. If we live according to our true nature and the created order, we will be happy. The primary instinct instilled in us by nature is the desire for self-preservation (*oikeiosis*). We ascribe value to aspects of life as being good if they enhance our constitution and bad if they detract from it. Unlike Aristotle's transcendent concept of the good, the Stoics centered the concept of good in the nature of things and how the good contributes to our constitution. Having a deterministic approach to nature, the Stoics viewed the good life as the cultivation of whatever would dispose people to live at peace with the world. Rather than change what is natural, we should adapt our emotions and behavior to conform. If we rationally do this, we will be happy and truly virtuous. The perfect sage is totally virtuous and therefore totally happy because he or she has accepted whatever circumstances occur and is not deterred by the unnatural and false temptations of the material world. Moral reflection for the Stoic is the rational process of saving the soul by aligning desires with nature's patterns and making choices that conform to those desires.

While Stoic influence waned after 300 CE, the concepts of our place in a deterministic natural order, the way in which moral virtue is tied to a self-controlled individual life, and the notion that the flourishing life is far more than superficial desires are themes that are frequently entertained throughout the history of economic thought and that are considered today by any modern economist reflecting on the connection between moral life and economic activity.

If the Greeks and Stoics were the secular thinkers and the Jews and Christians were the religious practitioners, the Romans were the secular doers. As empire builders and lawmakers, their control reached throughout the Mediterranean region and northern Africa and into northern Europe and present-day Ireland/Great Britain. A form of military pragmatism characterized their imperialism, and a majority of the population were slaves. However, they brought relative peace to the region for nearly five hundred years, and the average standard of living was improved over earlier periods in history. What worked to govern the empire dominated the Romans' thinking. Compared with the works of the Greek philosophers, moral reflection on economic and social issues was limited. Exceptions to this are found in Cato and other Roman rhetoricians, as well as in parts of Roman law that addressed economic activity. Until the fourth century, Christians in the empire were persecuted and kept from places where their moral reflection might have proved influential. With the toleration of the emperor Decius and the conversion of the emperor Constantine in 313 CE, the place of the church changed from being a persecuted enclave to a state-recognized entity. In the next chapter, we consider the influence of the Greek philosophers, Roman law, and changing circumstances in shaping the moral reflections of the medieval Scholastics on economic justice.

ARISTOTLE AND THE PURPOSE OF LIFE

When economists come to the question of what is the good life and how can people flourish and find it, we usually conclude that individuals decide what will make them happy and then optimize that happiness subject to whatever constraints exist in their life. We define happiness as utility, and each person has a utility function to optimize. Ethical behavior is action that follows the rules of the market game in which we operate to acquire the basket of goods that maximizes our utility.

This is quite different from the classical view of ethics and the flourishing life. For Aristotle, genuine fulfillment in life is achieved when we follow the purpose for which we were created. Every created entity has an anatomical structure and a set of instincts that point to its true purpose. For humanity, the unique quality of life is rationality. The purpose of human existence is to employ rationality judiciously and discover those habits and behaviors that are good. This search for appropriate behavior is found in the middle ground that exists between the extremes of any given area of life. Appropriate and rational consumption of food, for example, lies somewhere between what our appetite dictates and a diet aligned with being thin to the point of being unhealthy. Happiness is not consuming more than what is really good for us to live healthy and well, even though our preference at a given moment may be to eat more. This is not just a matter of short-term or long-term happiness. Rather, having rationally uncovered what is good for us, our maximum happiness now will come from eating practices that lead to some mean or middle ground between the extremes. What is rationally best and rationally practiced brings the greatest happiness now and over time.

Ethics in Aristotle's *Nicomachean Ethics* focuses on the establishment of those habits and practices in life that lead to true happiness, or eudemonia. The development of the virtues gives us the means to live in ways that optimize our happiness. Further, the Greeks focused on the good of the community rather than individual preferences. Temperance, courage, and justice are interdependent virtues that help the group achieve its purpose. The flourishing moral life encompasses far more than the maximization of utility as practiced by the self-maximizing economic person sometimes called *homo economicus* in economic theory.

Questions for Discussion

1. How would you define happiness in your experience?
2. In what sense are wealth and fame intermediate goods desired to achieve other ends?
3. If other ends are the goal, what are those ends and how do you know when you have reached a final good?
4. Do you see yourself as operating primarily as an individual in your maximization efforts, or do you feel a part of some group, such as a family or community, whose collective happiness is your greatest desire?
5. If the rational choice model of homo economicus works best to predict behavior, does that mean it is a good description of how people operate?

Chapter 3

Moral Reflection on Economic Justice in Scholastic Economic Thought

Economic thought developed in Europe in the era commonly known as the Middle Ages and largely due to the efforts of the Scholastics. The medieval Scholastics were theologians, canonists or church lawyers, and clerics who applied Christian principles to the economic concerns of Europe from roughly 700 to 1500 CE. These "Doctors of the Church" drew on several sources, including the Scriptures, canon law, Aristotle, Roman law, and the Patristics (or church fathers). One outstanding Patristic thinker was Saint Augustine. His notion of a Christian society as the city of God helped to sustain a semblance of a Christian vision throughout the period. Also, some Jewish and Arabic Muslim writings during this time brought Aristotelian philosophy into Christian Europe, and it is into this tradition that Thomas Aquinas, a Mendicant teacher of the thirteenth century, delved as he sought to enrich Christian teaching. His *Summa Theologica* was a monumental attempt at bringing together Christian theology, Aristotelian philosophy, and the slowly changing economic and cultural life of that period.

In the *Summa*, Aquinas provided moral reflections on economic matters such as justice in pricing and money lending with interest. His thoughts are best understood in light of the changes in European economic life that were evident in the thirteenth century. During the more than five hundred years previous, the social structure of the Middle Ages was quite simple by current standards. Agriculture was the primary occupation with some small craft shops in the towns. Most people did not trade regularly in the marketplace except when surpluses were generated that were not earmarked for the landowners or royalty. Serfs were allocated land and had some incentive to enhance production, but the obligations to the lords were heavy and tended to keep the serfs at subsistence level. However, by the thirteenth century, trade was more prevalent and a class of merchants arose as middlemen capitalizing on the gains from trade that exist when specialization occurs and surpluses are generated.

When this happens at least three new aspects of an economy develop. First, exchange prices begin to receive increased attention. Second, the role of the middleman or trader must be made clear. Third, a medium of exchange must be developed to facilitate exchanges. This third requirement creates additional issues when the medium of exchange can also serve as a store of value. It is now easier to build up wealth by saving, particularly when one is compensated for doing so by the payment of interest. In modern times, we recognize that interest derives from time preference differences, the productivity of capital, and a risk premium; however any one of these is sufficient to generate interest value. In a world with minimal capital, time preference differences and risk are sufficient to create interest payments. By the thirteenth century, these new economic forces were sufficiently strong to confront the Scholastics with the task of sorting out the ethical implications of these trends in economic life.

The medieval clerics responded with moral instruction to merchants, laborers, employers, borrowers, and lenders. Three categories impacting the moral teaching of the Scholastics will be discussed in this chapter. The first category seeks to discern the purpose of action in the marketplace. If a good or service fulfills its natural purpose, it is considered just and moral. The second category of moral reflection involves economic actions that are indifferent, without virtue or fraud and deception. Finally, moral behavior in exchange forbids those in stronger bargaining positions from taking advantage of their power. This practice of economic compulsion is prominent in medieval discussions of justice. These categories of moral judgment will be related to the market activity of buying, selling, and lending.

Drawing on the Scriptures, Aquinas and other Scholastics observed that, in Israel, compassion was to be shown in not taking interest from the poor (Exodus 22:25). According to B. T. Nelson (1969), in such a status-based society the taking of interest on loans was for the "others," those outside the covenant with Yahweh, but not for the "brothers" within the tribes of Israel who had covenanted with God to serve Him (Deuteronomy 23:19–20). Loans could be made at interest only to those outside the kin group.

In the Mediterranean world, reliance on the Roman legal tradition, technological changes, and the development of market institutions gradually eroded the influence of the traditional status-based exchange. This opened the door for accepting loans made at interest, though the Romans at times relied on interest-rate ceilings. Two elements inherited from the Roman legal code (particularly the code found in Justinian's *Institutes*) were particularly influential on Scholastic teachings about the exchange of products and the extension of credit.

First, Roman law depicted bargaining between equals as the basis for establishing a just price and a just wage (Noell 1998). Fair bargaining with mutual consent would achieve justice in exchange, similar to a decision by a court or legislative body. A key element in the Roman legal code was mutual consent. Where consent was lacking or fraud was present, economic injustice occurred. Where deceit came into play, the legal principle of *laesio enormis* was applied, which stated that the disadvantaged party was entitled to restitution if the exchange price varied from the just price by more than 50 percent. These principles from Roman law were found in Justinian's *Institutes* (Moyle).

The second element, particularly significant in regard to the moral evaluation of credit, was the Roman law's recognition of the contract of *mutuum*. The giving of a *mutuum*, as defined in the *Institutes*, occurs in the loan of those things that are made up by weight, number, or measure, such as wine, oil, grain, or money (Moyle, 130). In such transactions, the borrower is obliged to repay in goods only the exact amount of weight, number, or measure that he received. Additional fees would require a separate contract. The term used to describe such repayment was *usura* (Gordon 1975, 162).

It was the payment of usura that was problematic, for as Aquinas stated, money is a consumptible good (Aquinas, vol. 3, 1512–1513); it is "consumed in use and therefore has no use separate from its substance—and hence no use value" (Langholm 1998, 63). Because money was viewed as a natural medium of exchange and not a store of value, there was no legitimate basis for requiring interest to be paid on a loan.

As financial practices evolved with the commercial revolution in Europe in the thirteenth and fourteenth centuries, lending money at interest became more prevalent for both the "other" and the "brother." Aquinas and the other Scholastics struggled with the legitimacy of interest payments, but they were largely unwilling to recognize time preference as the basis for interest payments. Instead, following Aristotle's perspective, they grounded their prohibition of usury in the sterility of money and thus found the payment of interest to be "unnatural."

Aquinas was heavily influenced by Aristotle and his conception of what is natural. Finding the true purpose for exchange and then setting boundaries around exchange that would maintain that purpose was the way to make trade legitimate. The same is true for the lending of funds at interest and for pricing goods in a market. Consider Aquinas's effort to justify market transactions. He writes:

> First, as considered in themselves, and from this point of view, buying and selling seem to be established for the common advantage of both parties, one of whom requires that which belongs to the other, and vice versa....Now whatever is established for the common advantage, should not be more of a burden to one party than to another, and consequently all contracts between them should observe equality of thing and thing. Again, for this purpose money was invented....Therefore if either the price exceed the quantity of the thing's worth, or, conversely, the thing exceed the price, there is no longer the equality of justice: and consequently, to sell a thing for more than its worth, or to buy it for less than its worth, is in itself unjust and unlawful.
>
> (Aquinas, vol. 3, 1507)

The "quantity of the thing's worth" alluded to by Aquinas is often considered to be something approximating an equilibrium market price. However, making a simple equation of market equilibrium price and Aquinas's just price misses the nuances of balancing the benefits received by the consumer and the opportunities forgone by the seller.

Like Aristotle, Aquinas first seeks the primary purpose for which something is created. This is its real nature, its final cause, or its end. Once that end is determined, the proper moral safeguards are needed to be sure that the real nature is retained. As suggested by Aquinas, the purpose of trade is for the mutual benefit of each party. A genuinely mutual exchange would seem to involve equal net benefit for each person in the transaction, so that the exchange price divided the benefits of exchange equally. In modern terms, the consumer and producer surplus should be equally shared. Yet Aquinas recognized that often the best that could be hoped for in regard to dividing the exchange was to approximate equality. He affirms that divine law cannot determine the just price perfectly because "the just price of things is not fixed with mathematical precision, but depends on a kind of estimate" (Aquinas, vol. 3, 1508). The just price could vary depending on timing and setting. Institutionalized trading, relying on established markets and changing prices, was clearly a phenomenon the Scholastic writers had to account for in any formulation of the ethics of exchange. Kaye explains that they employed a conception of market pricing that apprehends "the shifting estimation of value in the marketplace, recognizes the varying effects of scarcity and need on changing prices, and accepts the necessity to anticipate and calculate in order to minimize loss and maximize gain" (Kaye, 378).

Aquinas's discussion of the just exchange is framed in terms of commutative justice. He is dealing with justice as "the relationship of one person to another, justice in a transaction between an individual seller and a single buyer in a particular market. Pricing is not considered in the wider context of the claims of distributive justice where the economic well-being of the community as a whole is a relevant reference point" (Gordon 1975, 177). Two requirements may be identified with respect to the Scholastic criteria for commutative justice. First, justice in exchange "cannot let a seller's (or a buyer's) greed run loose and influence price, either for his own sake or in view of the need of the opposite party to the exchange. But it must permit him to charge a price which preserves his economic incentive" (Langholm 1992, 573). Similarly, requirements were put on profits to give them legitimacy: "Merchants ought to strive to quench the avarice that threatened them and spend some of their honourably earned profit on charity" (Langholm 2003, 235). Yet Aquinas avoided appealing to the status of the participants in a particular exchange as the basis for setting the just price. Gordon rightly notes that, to Aquinas, "where actions are concerned, he is not prepared to differentiate between persons except as they act in a moral or immoral fashion in conduction of those transactions" (Gordon 1975, 178). Clearly coercion, deceit, or fraud in exchange constituted examples of immoral economic conduct which exhibit deviation from the true purpose of economic activity.

For the Scholastics, moral reasoning about usury and justice in exchange is not merely an abstract exercise. The standard of commutative justice is to be applied in everyday economic life. Determining the just price is a practical necessity for church clerics. Consider the discussion of economic justice in pricing in the penitential handbooks. As Langholm observes, "In these books, individual believers, including merchants, are examined and instructed regarding sin in general and with reference to their particular states and professions" (Langholm 2003, 3). Penance is to be applied to sins in the economic realm. One of the earliest examples of economic transgression pertains to the use of false weights and measures. Charlemagne's assembly of councils issues the decree that "weights and measures be everywhere equal and just, as stated in Lev.19:36 and Prov.20:10" (Langholm 2003, 18). By the thirteenth century, specific practices were banned in the handbooks such as "using different scales for buying and for selling, making one arm of the scales longer than the other, counting falsely, selling bad for good, a worthless substance for a precious one, a sick horse for a healthy one, rotten meat for fresh, soaking wool and certain spices to make them heavier, diluting wine or otherwise adulterating and mixing liquid goods, counterfeiting, clipping or otherwise mutilating coins, etc." (Langholm 2003, 238).Its not surprising then that a number of Scholastic works include in their theological commentary on the prohibition of theft in the Ten Commandments a discussion of fraud as representative of unjust pricing.

Likewise the Scholastic opposition to usury was in part linked to fraudulent practices. In the lending of funds, fraud could be committed when a borrower was misled by the lender as to the terms of the loan, or the lender was misled as to the borrower's intentions for the use of the funds and/or the ability to repay them.

In the absence of fraud, the Scholastics tended to emphasize the validity of prices and wages determined by the consent of both sides of the market. Yet the Scholastics qualified the place of consent that was so important for Roman law and for Augustine. Extreme poverty could put a buyer (or seller) in a desperate position so that there was radical disparity in bargaining power. The economic disadvantage due to need was recognized: "The idea that economic exchange can sometimes involve a certain element of coercion, even though no physical force is applied, appeared quite early on in the penitential literature. Peter the Chanter repeatedly refers to economic actors 'forced by need'" (Langholm 2003, 240). One party, in particular, needs to offer his consent to the transaction, yet "[h]is consent is then voluntary in a conditional sense only. To force such terms upon a needy buyer (or seller) by the exercise of bargaining power is prohibited by the moral law and the terms are unjust" (Langholm 1992, 578). Of course there are degrees of need as the Scholastics recognized. It should be noted that, for Gerald Odonis and Peter Olivi, "[n]eed is not compulsion as such; need is a particular kind of economic compulsion, different from but on a par with physical or moral compulsion" (Langholm 1982, 273–274).

This concept is applied in regard to consenting to borrowing funds at interest. For example, Thomas of Chobham challenges "the claims by some creditors that their debtors pay usury freely and willingly." Chobham asserts that "however much someone who has agreed to pay usury says that he gives the creditor something voluntarily, all the same he does not give it voluntarily of an absolute will but of a comparative will, because he wishes to give something, better than to be altogether without a loan" (quoted in Langholm 1992, 59). Numerous Scholastics including Aquinas make this distinction between a free-will choice and a forced choice because of a dismal alternative. The origins of this distinction are found in Aristotle, who discusses the issue of an economic act engaged in under compulsion in terms of a nautical example. The ship's captain, faced with a severe storm, must jettison cargo to prevent the ship from capsizing. He does so voluntarily, yet it is a qualified "voluntariness." Appealing to this example, Albert the Great states that the person who must pay usury pays it voluntarily only in the sense in which "the captain of a ship in peril jettisons cargo voluntarily" (Langholm 1992, 195). In the thirteenth century, "William of Auxerre reverses the direction of moral observation....While Aristotle's concern is a person's moral responsibility for his own actions, when performed under duress, William shifts the focus of the moral judgment to the person who deliberately imposes duress upon another, as in the case of the usurer refusing to lend without charge" (Langholm 1992, 80). Likewise in the fourteenth century, Antonino of Florence finds from his worldly experience that "people in need tend to affirm and put in writing whatever the usurer demands" (quoted in Langholm 1998, 66).

The thrust of Scholastic teaching on the economic duress associated with usury paid by the borrower underscores the fact that it eliminates the "bargaining between equals" fundamental to just transactions. Consequently, the moral teaching against usury continues through the Reformation. In three papers, Martin Luther strongly criticizes the taking of interest in a loan. In all these teachings, loans are viewed as consumption loans to the poor rather than loans made for productive capital. The productivity of capital had not yet been incorporated into the moral picture.

In the product market, Scholastics observed the presence of economic coercion where the poor were gouged by merchants who engaged in forestalling, regrating, or price discrimination. By forestalling, a merchant purchased a necessity before it reached a particular market in order to mark up its price; by regrating the trader simply purchased it in a given market in order to resell it at a higher price. As efforts to obtain monopolistic power, both practices are condemned by the Schoolmen. Price discrimination is also condemned; the Scholastics declared that "higher prices should not be charged from transients than from residents. Exploiting tourists is not a new phenomenon" (Langholm 2003, 242). By identifying these violations of justice, the Scholastics placed great weight on the obligations of market participants to act justly in exchange.

While the Scholastics could appeal to the significance of competition as a check on fraud or economic compulsion in product markets, no such appeal could be made for lending markets in the "coin economy" dominant throughout medieval Europe. Isolation from competition due to a scattered population and primitive means of communication enhanced the bargaining power of credit suppliers (Langholm 2003, 248). Lenders often acted either as local monopolists or in collusion. As Mews and Abraham observe, "the critique of usury by Franciscan and Dominican preachers in the 13th century was itself a reaction to often crippling interest rates being charged in urban centres" (Mews and Abraham).

The duty of the Christian lender or merchant to those of little means was a consistent theme among the Schoolmen and shaped their understanding of Christian freedom. The Christian lender is to pursue his duty to lend freely and not take advantage of his neighbor's need through usury. The Scholastics emphasized the personal accountability before God of each participant in the transaction.

While the thrust of Scholastic teaching on usury was focused on lenders making use of a superior bargaining position relative to borrowers in charging them interest, exceptions to the usury prohibition began to surface in Scholastic commentary in the thirteenth century. Recognition that default by borrowers significantly disadvantaged lenders led to some tolerance of the charging of interest. Scholastic thinkers began to permit "the use of legal exemptions, such as extrinsic titles, to evade" the label of usury (McGovern 1970). Extrinsic titles to interest came to be extended to "loss emerging in the case of delay, to profit forgone during the actual period of the loan, and the obligation to show opportunity and intent to actually use one's money in a specific way" (Langholm 1992, 592–593). Thus Aquinas offers the exception of *damnum emergens* in stating "[a] lender may without sin enter an agreement with the borrower for compensation for the loss he incurs of something he ought to have, for this is not to sell the use of money but to avoid a loss" (Aquinas, vol. 3, 1514). It was finally in the mid-sixteenth century that the Protestant reformer John Calvin reversed the direction of previous Scholastic thought on usury. Calvin affirmed the legitimacy of charging interest on loans but qualified his tolerance of usury by emphasizing the Deuteronomic ban on lending money at interest to the poor.

By the early fourteenth century, product markets widened as technological change facilitated a wider scope for the transportation of goods. Increased competition lessened the likelihood and degree of economic compulsion. Yet the question remained as to how to best measure the extent to which the weaker party was taken advantage of in the remaining instances of economic compulsion. In Scholastic thought, the standard would be provided by the competitive market price for the commodity. It serves as the standard of economic justice because it offers protection against economic compulsion. In the market, no one can force the price of individual transactions above or below market value, because there will be better alternatives. Competition among sellers protects buyers and vice versa (Langholm 1998b, 469), and the market price could function as a standard of comparison: "A hypothetical competitive market price, estimated by a good and experienced man, or by the priest or the penitents themselves, might serve as a benchmark from which to measure the amount of ill-gotten gains to be restored or to be given in alms" (Langholm 2003, 248). Confessional handbooks reference the market price because of its role in protecting against economic compulsion (Langholm 2003, 247). The emphasis on competition was heightened by those referred to as the late Scholastics of the sixteenth and seventeenth centuries.

In the late sixteenth century, the Scholastic writers placed less emphasis on the personal duties associated with exchange. As exchange itself became less personalized with wider markets, economic thought shifted its focus "from the moral quality of individual exchanges to the socially beneficial effects of suprapersonal economic mechanisms" (Langholm 1992, 577). Thus there was less rationale for interfering with exchanges based on consent. This element of the evolving economic justice doctrine is evident in the qualifications issued by the late Scholastics. For example, the Spanish Scholastic cardinal Cajetan argues that any price, even a just price, can be claimed by the buyer or the seller to have been paid or accepted involuntarily, because better alternatives were not available to them. However low the price paid, the buyer would have preferred a lower one; however high, the seller would have preferred a higher one (Langholm 2003, 243).

Dominican friars such as Cajetan were much less concerned with personal motivations for selling and purchasing. Instead they referred the actions of poor and rich alike to broader market forces and thus heralded a new way of economic reasoning through which poverty and need are remedied by the market and the individual is subsumed in the aggregate forces of supply and demand (Langholm 2003, 249). Thus in late Scholastic thinking there is a greater acceptance of the impersonal forces of competition in both product and labor markets. The legacy they created was modified by Adam Smith in the eighteenth century when he discussed how competition limited the practice of economic compulsion. Smith's analysis of the conditions for the payment of a living wage is an extension of late Scholastic thought on the justice of labor market exchanges (Noell 2006).

Like their predecessors, the late Scholastics emphasized the significance of competitive employment opportunities. A just wage is paid as a consequence of a worker seeking the best job opportunities in an extensive labor market. In the early seventeenth century, the Belgian Jesuit Leonard Lessius described how a floor for the just wage is determined: "It can be established that [the wage payment] is not below the minimum from the fact that there are others who are willing to perform such work or office or service for the remuneration in question. That is a clear indication that such remuneration, all circumstances considered, is not below the right value for that occupation" (quoted in Gordon 1975, 263). Despite this trust in the impersonal market both the late Scholastics and their contemporaries the Protestant Reformers still highlight the personal accountability of labor market participants to the Creator and to each other (Noell 2001).

Moral reflection by Scholastic writers aimed at the achievement of economic justice in line with Christian values in product, labor, and loanable funds markets. As Kaye observes, "the primary question scholastic thinkers asked concerning economic activity was not 'how does it work?' but 'what is permitted and what is not? what is sinful and what is not?'" (Kaye 1998, 79). They sought what was natural and just, a concept that depended on needs and a meaningful subsistence for all involved. Provision of these needs was the first goal of economic life and thus the primary concern of moral reflection. If market forces pulled price away from serving this goal, it was condemned. If the goal was met and there was still surplus value, the scholastics were inclined to let the market price allocate the surplus. The Scholastics understood that bargaining that comes to consent does not mean either party has abandoned reciprocity. The medieval theologians who were increasingly tolerant of market exchange recognized that elements of gift giving remained. When two parties have bargained and reach an agreed-on transaction price, it is the consequence of bargaining in which each must yield from his reservation price: "In the end each will settle somewhat below his own estimate. There is thus an element of gift in economic exchange, from both parties" (Langholm 1992, 576). Moreover, the element of duty is central in the Scholastic conception of justice in exchange. The Schoolman taught that Christians must avoid avarice and freely share as their duty to God.

The Scholastics understood the social virtue of economic incentive and to some extent acknowledged the practical and moral advantages of free bargaining. Yet for a Christian ethic, the social aspect is secondary because the primary focus must remain with the duties of each person encountering his neighbor in the context of exchange, to combat his greed and to relieve the economic need of his neighbor (Langholm 1992, 577–578).

In summarizing Scholastic thought on economic activity, we recognize they operate with three categories from which moral reflection takes place. The first is the category of high virtue where the natural purpose is served and where equal net benefit results from the act. The second category, called *adiaphora* by the Scholastics, is one in which behavior is neither sinful nor virtuous. This concerns areas where the process is unnatural but the appropriate end is served. An example of this would be trading for profit but helping the poor with the proceeds. Finally, there is the unnatural, sinful act of using the gains for personal benefit beyond basic needs without any consideration of reciprocity. When viewed through a modern lens with the concept of natural purpose (or telos) filtered out and where sinful economic transactions seem irrelevant in voluntary markets, it is easy to collapse all three categories into one value-free notion of supply and demand. It is then a short step to the argument that the Scholastic writers were really talking about a "neutral" market price all along, which discounts or overlooks the context of their work and the moral content of their analysis.

Instead, one must recognize that Scholastic thought reflected the extension and development of concepts found in their authoritative sources (particularly the Scriptures, Patristics, canon law, and Aristotle) regarding the ultimate purpose of economic activity and finding ways to accomplish economic justice. They started from human nature as they found it to be and reflected on human behavior as it should be if it recognized its true telos. Through synthesizing the teaching of the authoritative sources, they then derived ethical and moral standards to try to bring the two disparate conditions together. All social, political, economic, and religious analysis was to be integrated by moral reflection and discernment. But as time moved on, with the influence of some facets of Enlightenment thinking, moralizing about economic behavior seemed to stand in the way of progress in economic affairs, and moralizing did not seem to fit the way people actually behaved when given opportunities for advancement. The next chapter considers the work of Adam Smith, a Scottish Enlightenment philosopher-economist who still viewed economics as a moral science. Chapter 5 describes the shift to a fact/value dichotomy and a value-free economics which occured after Smith's death.

MEDIEVAL SCHOLASTICS AND MORAL VALUES FOR THE SUBPRIME MORTGAGE CRISIS

The financial crisis of 2008–2009 brought to light some dubious behavior in financial markets. Some of the most egregious practices were found in the subprime mortgage loan market. Subprime borrowers have low or unpredictable incomes and typically do not have a down payment of at least 20 percent of the dwelling's value. Their total monthly housing payment exceeds a reasonable fraction, such as 30 percent, of the family's monthly income. Many obtain adjustable-rate mortgages in which a low "teaser" interest rate is charged for several years, after which the interest rate rises substantially. Various accounts from the financial press indicate subprime mortgage loans were sometimes accompanied by the following practices: doctored incomes and/ or lack of verification of an applicant's income on loan application forms; appraisal fraud countenanced by borrowers and lenders alike; borrowers being offered "pick a payment" loans for which the lowest mortgage payment did not even cover the interest on the loan; and borrowers taking out several loans in the space of a few years to take advantage of selling houses quickly in the midst of rising housing prices.

Insights derived from Scholastic reflections on usury, avarice, and unjust gain can be helpful in thinking about the moral dimensions of these credit market practices. While any ban on interest on mortgage loans is not feasible, there is merit in considering how the Scholastics emphasize the role of personal moral agency in matters of lending and borrowing funds. Certainly one might defend subprime mortgage loans in that they no doubt help make houses affordable which would otherwise be prohibitive for many lower-income families via the traditional thirty-year fixed-rate mortgage. Yet one should surely also carefully the practice of excessive borrowing by speculators who sought to turn over houses to take advantage of the increased opportunity to borrow easily in the subprime market.

Scholastic ethics also focus on "predatory practices" by subprime mortgage lenders with respect to more vulnerable borrowers in society. Mortgage lenders are often driven by the incentive for gain from an increased volume of loans generated. What should be highlighted is the role of deceit and the extent to which subprime borrowers are misled in taking out loans with low prospects of repayment and little collateral required. If these examples do not necessarily entail borrowing out of economic desperation, they do at least raise the specter of a borrower's regret at taking on a loan under pressure or because of misleading information from the agent in the process.

Of course not all subprime mortgage loans are predatory loans. Moreover, modern usury laws create credit market shortages and often only make it more difficult for low-income borrowers to obtain loans. Yet policy practices reflecting Scholastic values would institute greater transparency in lending as they call us to consider more carefully the extent to which ignorance and dire need can be exploited by lenders.

Questions for Discussion

1. How might mortgage brokers be given greater incentive to insure that borrowers are creditworthy and to provide fuller transparency in lending?

2. To what extent should speculative borrowers be forced to bear the consequences of their actions?

3. Will a government bailout of subprime mortgage lenders and/ or borrowers simply increase people's belief that they can make risky decisions and not have to face the consequences? Why or why not?

Chapter 4

Adam Smith and the Prospects for Moral Reflection in Enlightenment Thinking

In much of the discussion so far, moral reflection has been related to a sense of telos or the purpose to which human action is directed. Only when there is a goal can there be a meaningful discussion about what is right and wrong or good and bad. Even if the goal is simply to be what one is intended to be, as Aristotle might say, there is a good and bad way of attempting to reach the goal because the source of the intention must come from outside the person involved. Moral dialogue is important to discern what behavior is appropriate, and so any effort to pursue one's purpose involves moral reflection. When a process lacks intentionality and can be explained as a mechanistic system there is no need for moral discernment. When Isaac Newton postulated the universe as a mechanism where mass followed certain rules of motion perpetually, no purpose was attributed to the motion, and therefore moral reflection about the mechanism would be meaningless. The key question became: Is an economic system like a machine, or does it require moral dialogue to function well? For centuries this question was at the forefront of social system analysis, and in many ways it still persists.

One of the foremost thinkers of the eighteenth century was Adam Smith, who painstakingly constructed a vision of political economy that blended a mechanistic scientific system with a moral one. This chapter is primarily about Smith, and it attempts in some detail to describe his moral philosophy; but before looking at his work it is important to briefly review some of the tension of the times in which he worked. It took centuries for the medieval world-view to evolve toward democratic capitalism. Simple inventions brought increases in output that stressed the longstanding distribution norms. Using four-wheeled wagons, replacing oxen with horses, employing a three-crop rotation rather than the two-crop practice brought growth in production that had not occurred routinely before. Leaving half the land fallow each year would result in half a crop, but leaving only one-third fallow would yield two-thirds of a full crop. This is an 18 percent increase in production assuming the change did not deteriorate the soil. Dividing the increase stressed the social system and resulted in peasant uprisings, while dissatisfaction with the conservative nature of the church-state coalition led to increased support for new ways of thinking about the social order. Martin Luther and the reformers of the early sixteenth century promoted a more individualized faith that seemed compatible with a system that relied more on market outcomes than on traditional ways of allocating resources.

In short, the forces of technology and the reformation slowly ushered in a new kind of world where religion was more privatized and independent of the state and the economy was viewed increasingly as a product of natural, impersonal forces rather than moral principles. The separation of church and state did not come easily even in the United States, where many faith-based groups sought freedom of religion but all groups were not granted equal rights. The First Amendment rights of freedom of religion in the U.S. Constitution were granted only after intense battles between dominant and growing religious groups. In England at the time, shops and small factories were generating output that led to rapid economic growth. Specialization and trade made many traditional forms of economic life obsolete. The times called for new ideas and a more unifying vision for society. Integrating economics, politics, and the moral life into a single social order was a daunting task. From the Enlightenment period onward, most efforts to build a workable system focused on a value-free scientific economic system with supportive political institutions, while moral reflection was relegated to private musings. However, Adam Smith was unwilling to ignore the moral life in his understanding of how the world worked, but it is not always clear how his moral theory and his economic theory are connected because in his political economy book on The *Wealth of Nations* he never refers to his earlier work on *The Theory of Moral Sentiments*. This has caused some to believe that Smith separated economics and moral dialogue. Vivienne Brown reads Adam Smith's work as involving a positive and normative dichotomy similar to the modern approach to economic thinking (Brown, 1991). She sees two levels at work in the way Smith deals with the human passions. It is the passions of the upper tier of beneficence and self-command that require moral dialogue and fit the area that contemporary economists call normative economics. On the other hand, justice and prudence are subject to rules of the system, which is mechanistically ordered and therefore naturally separated from moral dialogue. The pursuit of self-interest is part of this lower mechanistic order and therefore is amoral in nature. In Brown's words:

> But the crucial point is that the virtue of economic self-interest
> is treated differently in [*The Theory of Moral Sentiments*] from
> the higher moral virtues of beneficence and self-command,
> the true objects of moral discourse as defined by the structure

of the argument in TMS, and it is this differential treatment
in the TMS itself that signals a different moral status for [*The
Wealth of Nations*], a difference epitomized by the absence of
the impartial spectator from the pages of the WN.

(Brown, 210–211)

Thus Brown sees Smith's imaginative concept of the impartial
spectator as the normative side of Smith as seen in *The Theory of
Moral Sentiments* (*TMS*), and she sees his concept of approbation
as the positive mechanistic component of economic analysis shown
in *An Inquiry into the Nature and Causes of the Wealth of Nations*
(*WN*). Smith led the way to establishing the notions of positive and
normative economics, in positive economics there being no room
for moral dialogue. Brown argues that any effort to superimpose
TMS on the *WN* in order to make the two blend together is a futile
project.

It is not the purpose of this chapter to systematically debate
Brown's work. Richard Kleer has critiqued Brown's claims in a subsequent article (Kleer, 1993). Rather, what follows is an attempt to
show that the concept of telos informed Smith's work and that for
him moral reflection is assumed to be part of any economic thinking. A case will be made that Smith did not separate fact and value
as many contemporary economists do. Nevertheless, it is recognized that Smith may have been conflicted over time in his effort
to follow a path between the moral sense teaching of his mentor
Francis Hutcheson and the neoskeptical influence of his friend
David Hume.

Smith has been recognized as one of the most astute analysts of
economic behavior despite the fact that his work was done before
the Industrial Revolution reached its full bloom. He is not easy
to categorize because of the many influences that were at work in
his thinking. Significant to his moral theory is the influence of the

Stoic tradition reaching back to the Greeks. The label *deist* is most commonly applied to Smith's philosophical and religious posture, since he sees the creator as a benevolent force in the order of things. Critical of organized religion, his revisions of the *TMS* show a drift some distance away from any appreciation of the truth claims of Christianity as he observed it.

The reading of Smith that we propose is one that sees him as conflicted about religion and the source of moral life. He was deeply concerned that society develop a vision of how people ought to be and that the source of that vision should be ultimately placed outside the individual. We will argue that Smith is an intermediary between the premodern world, where the existence of a telos was assumed, and the modern world, where a purpose for life outside a person's individual preference is considered irrelevant. Smith's work in moral philosophy was an attempt to show the moral process that was needed to control human passions so that a higher moral purpose could be reached. In economic life, the issue is whether the market is socialized effectively by self-interest mediated by competition and innate moral impulses or whether the market needs an ongoing moral dialogue to make it work well. Are nature's checks on bad behavior routine and mechanical, or do they require continual attention in order to be effective? Such attention takes the form of a moral dialogue that must reference some sense of human telos.

How a modern economist comes at this question will be different from Smith's approach. In the time in which Smith worked, Christianity's heavy moral hand on commerce was just beginning to fall away. Its impact had been fairly restrictive, as some commercial activity had been considered questionable or even sinful. Smith's views had the effect of replacing Christian theology with a Stoic form of natural theology. If Smith was going to err in his efforts, he would most likely have wanted to do so by downplaying anything that looked like religious moral restraint. On the other hand, modern economists work in a methodology that claims to be value free. They are inclined to see moral issues and notions of virtue as existing outside economic thinking altogether. Putting these two tendencies together, it is fair to conclude that most interpretations of Smith's work will lean in the direction of finding a minimum of moral reflection in it. In short, present-day economists, who see no role for moral reflection in economic analysis, when interpreting Smith, who was trying to move economics away from oppressive moral rules, will quite easily see an absence of telos in his work.

Smith's moral philosophy and his notion of natural theology deserve scrutiny as well. The *TMS* is a delight to read, and it puts the reader in touch with his or her own feelings because many of the case examples Smith uses are common to everyone. There is no debate that he sees behavior as motivated more by the passions, which include emotions, imagination, and instincts, than by rational cost-benefit calculations. Nature has instilled in people the necessary ingredients to make society viable and flourishing. They are the subject of any fruitful analysis of human behavior, including economic behavior. The key ingredient given by nature is the desire to maintain one's own life and, secondarily, the lives one cares most about. Rationality is merely a tool to fulfill that primary passion. Joseph Cropsey relates Smith's view of the passions and reason by claiming that

> [N]ature provides man with imperfect perceptions of the tangible world, with the inevitable result that he can reason only imperfectly concerning the nature of things or what they really are. The faculty of reason leans upon an aid which was prepared by nature to assist not reason but appetite, specifically the appetite for life as such; and as a result, useful knowledge but not real knowledge is the most that man can aspire to.
>
> (Cropsey, 8)

Thus appetites and passions determine behavior, but for Smith they need moral restraint or direction if they are to serve the goal of self-preservation. We now turn to Smith's moral philosophy, which socializes the passions and makes them fit servants of the goal of self-preservation.

Sympathy: The First Moral Screen of Behavior

Contemporary economic theory tends to isolate the individual economic consumer from the influence of others. Preferences of the consumer are viewed as exogenous to the system, and little if any interdependence is considered. Where interdependence is considered, the straightforward predictions of traditional theory become problematic. Bandwagon effects, where people desire what is popular, or snob effects, where extravagance elevates social standing, play havoc with demand functions. In cases like this, rational choice outcomes can be altered and cooperative behavior rather than individual behavior may be the best way to achieve certain goals. Maintaining an independent *homo economicus* may keep the analysis manageable but causes it to miss out on many aspects of human behavior.

Smith's analysis was not limited in this way. From the beginning, Smith assumes people are interdependent in their feelings for one another. Because people share similar feelings and passions, they can identify with others as they express their passions through their behavior. This identification Smith called sympathy, and it is deeply rooted in our being. "By the imagination we place ourselves in his situation, we conceive ourselves enduring all the same torments, we enter as it were into his body, and become in some measure the same person with him, and thence form some idea of his sensations, and even feel something which, though weaker in degree, is not altogether unlike them" (Smith, *TMS*, 9).

The instinct of sympathy is not a rational transporting of one into another's existence. Rather, it is a built-in response that is, for the most part, involuntary. If I watch a football game in which my alma mater or favorite professional team is playing, I find that I have an unconscious response that illustrates sympathy behavior. If my team has a fourth down and goal at the 1-yard line and the play called is a plunge up the middle, I find myself physically leaning toward the goal during the play, even though there is no rational reason for such action. I simply am identifying strongly enough with the particular play that my senses respond. If I were running the ball, I would be straining every muscle to reach the goal. Smith's example is similar: "When we see a stroke aimed and just ready to fall upon the leg or arm of another person we naturally shrink and draw back our own leg or our own arm; and when it does fall, we feel it in some measure and are hurt by it as well as the sufferer" (Smith, *TMS*, 10).

Smith illustrates the sympathy concept by giving a comprehensive dose of real-life situations in order to tease out of the reader a common sense notion of this identification process. The *TMS* is largely given to an analysis of various human passions and how they are conditioned by sympathy. This quality of sympathy impacts all of our passions in one way or another.

Smith begins the *TMS* by pointing to deeply innate social passions that exist in everyone no matter how antisocial one may appear. He notes: "How selfish soever man may be supposed, there are evidently some principles in his nature, which interest him in the fortunes of others, and render their happiness necessary to him, though he derives nothing from it except the pleasure of seeing it" (Smith, *TMS*, 9). The passions of pity and compassion for someone in dire circumstances illustrate how one's happiness is reduced by observing distress or pain in another person. Conversely, the alleviation of such pain enhances our pleasure. This consideration of others occurs because of the ability to assess how we would feel if we were in the suffering person's place. This exercise of our social passions through sympathy is the most meritorious behavior possible in our state of mutual interdependence.

Smith recognized these benevolent affections as inborn, and he included generosity, compassion, benevolence, and esteem as part of these social passions that represented humanity at its best:

> And hence it is, that to feel much for others and little for ourselves, that to restrain our selfish, and to indulge our benevolent affections, constitutes the perfection of human nature; and can alone produce among mankind that harmony of sentiments and passions in which consists their whole grace and propriety. As to love our neighbor as we love ourselves is the great law of Christianity, so it is the great precept of nature to love ourselves only as we love our neighbor, or what comes to the same thing, as our neighbour is capable of loving us.
>
> (Smith, *TMS*, 25)

If the desire to care for others were all that human nature instills in people, there would be little need for moral dialogue since we would all naturally act in morally desirable ways. However, Smith recognized that these passions were only part of the complex makeup of people. He felt they were the weaker passions and therefore they could not make the social system viable.

The selfish passions are harder to socialize, but nature has not left us hopeless. Building on the notion that we have that fellow feeling called sympathy, two other features of our makeup are helpful in the socialization process. First, our sympathy for others is conditioned by the context involved. "Even our sympathy with the grief or joy of another, before we are informed of the cause of either, is always imperfect.... Sympathy therefore does not arise so much from the view of the passion, as from that of the situation which excites it" (Smith, *TMS*, 11–12). Second, we seek the approval or approbation of others because we are social beings. "But whatever may be the cause of sympathy, or however it may be excited, nothing pleases us more than to observe in other men a fellow feeling with all the emotions of our own breast" (Smith, *TMS*, 13).

Smith elaborates at length on the nuances of sympathy by including many examples of the selfish passions including pain, pleasure, joy, and self-preservation. The control of these passions is the key to the social viability of any society, and so it is important that others can see through the selfish passions enough to evaluate them and provide a corrective screen against the misuse of those passions. Clearly, Smith's notion of self-interest is not expressed as the isolated preference of an independent economic agent but rather as the conditioned response of an interdependent participant in a social process. The interdependent nature of sympathy allows this screen to function effectively. As Pat Werhane (1991) points out, even the butcher and the baker in the oft-used quote in the *WN* cannot ignore the preferences and expectations of people when they pursue their own interest in the restaurant. They are actually operating in a social environment that relies heavily on the interdependence inherent in sympathy and the judgment of the impartial spectator (IS). But still the question remains: Are these forces mechanical or subject to moral reflection?

The following example will help to flesh out the discussion so far. On a recent golf outing one of us experienced, as an observer, a sympathetic response to the passion of joy. A stranger, after making a long putt on another green, began shouting, dancing, and celebrating, finally jumping into another golfer's arms. My reaction was unfavorable because his joy seemed excessive. I made that judgment based on what I imagined I would do had I made a long putt. I would pump my fist once and make a celebratory comment as if I expected the putt to drop. I believe my playing partners would not be impressed if I was more effusive. Thus my judgment of the happy golfer's behavior requires that I, first, have the ability to put myself in that person's situation and mindset and imagine what my response would be if I made a long putt. I must also be able to imagine what the golfer's playing partners might think of the celebration. Finally, I would need to know the circumstances of the putt. If the putt was for a million dollars, my attitude would change quickly and the exuberant behavior would seem appropriate. This example illustrates Smith's concept of sympathy as an initial filter or first screen that moderates the passions. Embedded in this concept is a subtle qualifier to the notion of selfishness as it is commonly used. While the putter's passion might desire an outburst of extreme joy, his instincts should tell him what others consider sensible if they were in his place. The ability to be in sympathy with another is to go beyond personal boundaries and interests to a sense of what is appropriate for social harmony in a given context. In this story, I did not know whether the golfer was engaged in improper celebrating because I was not aware of the full context of the putt. Smith would expect the golfer to be able to predict the reaction of his peers and condition his behavior accordingly.

Unfortunately, sympathy has a down side. There are tendencies in human nature that can cause the group to approve of behavior that is morally questionable. One of the most pervasive examples of this problem in Smith's work is the manner in which we elevate the rich and disdain the poor. He notes: "It is because mankind are disposed to sympathize more entirely with our joy than with our sorrow, that we make parade of our riches, and conceal our poverty" (Smith, *TMS*, 50). This theme recurs regularly, assuming a pejorative tone toward those with great wealth: "This disposition to admire and almost to worship the rich and powerful, and to despise, or at least, to neglect persons of poor and mean conditions, though necessary both to establish and to maintain the distinction of ranks and the order of society, is, at the same time, the great and most universal cause of the corruption of our moral sentiments" (Smith, *TMS*, 9).

To make matters worse, this natural tendency in humans is reinforced by social norms that lend it credence:

> We desire both to be respectable and to be respected. We dread both to be contemptible and to be contemned. But upon coming into this world we soon find that wisdom and virtue are by no means the sole objects of respect; nor vice and folly, of contempt. We frequently see the respectful attentions of the world more strongly directed towards the rich and the great, than towards the wise and the virtuous. We see frequently the vices and follies of the powerful much less despised than the poverty and weakness of the innocent. To deserve, to acquire, and to enjoy the respect and admiration of mankind, are the great objects of ambition and emulation. Two different roads are presented to us, equally leading to the attainment of this so much desired object; the one by the study of wisdom and the practice of virtue; the other by the acquisition of wealth and greatness.
>
> (Smith, *TMS*, 62)

Smith is clear about which road he believes tends to dominate for those capable of traveling on it:

> To attain to this envied situation, the candidates for fortune too frequently abandon the paths of virtue; for unhappily, the road which leads to the one, and that which leads to the other, lie sometimes in very opposite directions. But the ambitious

man flatters himself that, in the splendid situation to which he advances, he will have so many means of commanding the respect and admiration of mankind, and will be enabled to act with such superior propriety and grace, that the lustre of his future conduct will entirely cover, or efface, the foulness of the steps by which he arrived at that elevation.

(Smith, *TMS*, 64)

Thus sympathy alone, for all its social usefulness, can not ensure moral outcomes. These lengthy quotations illustrate the high level of interdependency Smith saw in human behavior. They also reveal that he did not believe that approbation, fellow feeling, and approval seeking would be enough to maintain a moral and just social order. The dark side of human nature seemed to overpower the virtuous side too frequently. This darker side of human nature is seen most in the exercise of the selfish passions consisting of self-preservation, grief, joy, and pain/pleasure choices. These passions can have both positive and negative effects. On the other hand, the unsocial passions of hate, envy, and revenge are generally socially destructive so the moral screen of sympathy will control these passions.

The Impartial Spectator: The Second Moral Screen of Behavior

Since sympathy is not sufficient to socially condition the selfish passions, these passions need another safeguard. Smith realized that there needed to be a standard beyond one's built-in capacity to sympathize since the reference point for sympathy is one's own experience and since our natural sympathies are sometimes diverted from the virtuous. This safeguard for Smith is the impartial spectator.

Moral discernment requires a stronger foundation than a simple desire to be praised as illustrated by the example of how we treat the rich. To be truly moral is to develop the ability to do what is right rather than simply what is considered acceptable by the masses. In order to do right,

> I divide myself, as it were, into two persons; and that I, the examiner and judge, represent a different character from that other I, the person whose conduct is examined into and judged of. The first is the spectator, whose sentiments with regard to my own conduct I endeavour to enter into, by placing myself in his situation, and by considering how it would appear to me, when seen from that particular point of view. The second is the agent, the person whom I properly call myself, and of whose conduct, under the character of a spectator, I was endeavouring to form some opinion.
>
> (Smith, *TMS*, 114)

Operating as the first "I" in the situation described here is to tap into the moral discernment of the IS. The perspective of this observer helps one see what is praiseworthy and virtuous. For example, the exuberant golfer who received the forced praise from his partner, upon reflection, would want to know how praiseworthy his accomplishment really was before he judged his own response to the successful long putt. For that perspective, he should not look to his partner, who perhaps had a stake in the matter or was influenced by jealousy, but rather to someone who had no stake in the outcome and who knew all the circumstances. Such an impartial spectator would give a better reading of just how praiseworthy the accomplishment was. Smith presumed that people were capable of stepping outside themselves and going beyond mere sympathy to make an impartial assessment that considered all aspects of the behavior. In the golf story, the IS would factor out the jealousy and the emotion of the partner who, in this story, was assumed to be less fortunate in his putting. Instead, the IS would factor in what people might see from a distance in order to help the person arrive at an appropriate response to the situation. The same process of sympathy and the appropriation of the IS would be followed by the partner, and the end result would be behavior by both individuals that was just and prudent. Since most of this process is instinctual and done almost instantly, there is no observable moral dialogue. Thus it is easy to see this process as natural and mechanical rather than morally reflective.

However, something inside a person causes him or her to avoid undue praise. The motivation for good behavior is the built-in desire of people to be worthy of praise, not just praised for its own sake. In the same manner, if blamed, one expects to be truly blameworthy. "Man naturally desires, not only to be loved, but to be lovely; or to be that thing which is the natural and proper object of love. He naturally dreads, not only to be hated, but to be hateful; or to be that thing which is the natural and proper object of hatred" (Smith, *TMS*, 114). Blame that is known to be unworthy does not inflict as much harm as deserved blame, and praise that is unworthy does not gratify as much as praise that is worthy. The difference between the worthy and unworthy is discerned by the impartial spectator. To be virtuous is to be praiseworthy and to avoid being worthy of blame. A person whose passions are channeled effectively by sympathy and the IS is truly virtuous.

Smith has many examples of how this principle works. People who use makeup to cover a bad complexion are not genuinely flattered by compliments on their good skin. Alternatively, people who perform heroic acts do so recognizing that they may not live to receive any praise. People in their best moments seek what is virtuous, but the origin of this spectator on whom we rely to discern virtue is still somewhat ambiguous. Does it represent humanity as it ought to be if it recognized its true telos, or is it little more than the polling of an impartial audience at a game show?

Smith declares, "Man is the immediate judge of mankind, but an appeal comes from the higher tribunal of their own consciences, to that of the supposed impartial and well-informed spectator, to that of the man within the breast, the great judge and arbiter of their conduct" (Smith, *TMS*, 130). The lower and higher tribunals relate respectively to the desire to be praised and the desire to be praiseworthy. Peer judgments relate to the desire to be praised, but the impartial spectator calls us to desire the virtue of being praiseworthy. The creator has endowed all humans with both of these tribunals as complementary screens of behavior. The lower tribunal deals with the behavior itself and whether it is generally agreeable to others. The higher tribunal deals with the motives behind the action and the sincerity of the action. Smith states, "The man who is conscious to himself that he has exactly observed those measures of conduct which experience informs him are generally agreeable, reflects with satisfaction on the propriety of his own behaviour. When he views it in the light in which the impartial spectator would view it, he thoroughly enters into all the motives which influenced it" (Smith, *TMS*, 116).

In addition to dealing with the inner motivations of our actions, the IS helps condition our perspective, which is influenced by our interests, so that the larger social interest results. In an extended example, Smith tells of a person who injures his finger on the same day that China is ravaged by an earthquake. While the self-interest of the injured person is to complain about his finger, he comments to his neighbors on the horror of the earthquake instead. Smith asks the obvious question:

> When our passive feelings are almost always so sordid and so
> selfish, how comes it that our active principles should often be

so generous and so noble? ... It is not the soft power of humanity, it is not that feeble spark of benevolence which Nature has
lighted up in the human heart, that is thus capable of counter-
acting the strongest impulses of self love. It is a stronger power,
a more forcible motive, which exerts itself upon such occasions.
It is reason, principle, conscience, the inhabitant of the breast,
the man within, the great judge and arbiter of our conduct. It
is he who, whenever we are about to act so as to affect the happiness of other, calls to us, with a voice capable of astonishing
the most presumptuous of our passions, that we are but one of
the multitude, in no respect better than any other in it; and that
when we prefer ourselves so shamefully and so blindly to others, we become the proper objects of resentment abhorrence,
and execration.

(Smith, *TMS*, 137)

For Smith, there appears to be a private self-interest and a
social interest with the impartial spectator drawing humanity
away from the private to the social. The recognition that we are
social beings is a powerful one in Smith's thinking, but this passage implies that this social awareness is, in some way, instinctive in our human nature and, in another way, outside our nature.
Herein lies the difficulty in determining the role of moral reflection in Smith's work.

The teaching of the philosophers as to how we should act as
world citizens does not impress Smith. Here he is critical of even
the Stoics who try to "have us feel for all others as we naturally
feel for ourselves" (Smith, *TMS*, 139). For Smith, there is a natural
inequality of our passive feelings, and propriety merely calls us to
recognize how little we hurt when someone unknown to us suffers
so that we can better respond when we face similar circumstances
and do not receive the outpouring of emotion that is commensurate

to our own pain. In this case, there appears to be natural tendencies toward morality rather than direction based on moral reflection. In fact, the reflections of the moralists seem not to be helpful. In reflecting further on how we respond to distant situations, Smith is even more skeptical of philosophical reflection, writing:

> If we examine the different shades and gradations of weakness and self-command, as we meet with them in common life, we shall very easily satisfy ourselves that this control of our passive feelings must be acquired, not from the abstruse syllogisms of a quibbling dialectic, but from that great discipline which Nature has established for the acquisition of this and of every other virtue; a regard to the sentiments of the real or supposed spectator of our conduct.
>
> (Smith, *TMS*, 145)

These shades of weakness and self-command start with the weakest children who learn about sympathy and the approbation of others by experience. Adults with "little firmness" learn from the real spectator's expression of sympathy and it is a more enduring lesson, while the "man of real constancy and firmness" conditions his behavior so effectively, according to the wishes of both the real and supposedly impartial spectator, that he becomes the kind of person the impartial spectator is. "He does not merely affect the sentiments of the impartial spectator. He really adopts them. He almost identifies himself with, he almost becomes himself that impartial spectator, and scarce even feels but as that great arbiter of his conduct directs him to feel" (Smith, *TMS*, 147). From these two quotations it is clear that these screens of behavior are not founded in reason and philosophical discussion, and there is a progression to higher levels of moral stature. Nature prescribes the content of the IS, but people must still appropriate what nature has made available. This appropriation process is made possible by a Stoic view of self-control that eventually conditions a person's preferences to become one with the impartial spectator's perspective.

But people often do not possess constancy and firmness, so the moral battle is ever present. In one example of a person in distress, Smith describes the battle that goes on between the selfish passions and the IS:

> His own natural feelings of his own distress,...presses hard upon him, and he cannot, without a very great effort, fix his attention upon that of the IS. Both views present themselves to him at the same time. His sense of honour, his regard to his own dignity, directs him to fix his whole attention upon the one view. His natural, his untaught and undisciplined feelings, are continually calling it off to the other. He does not, in this case, perfectly identify himself with the ideal man within the breast, he does not become himself the impartial spectator of his own conduct.
>
> (Smith, *TMS*, 148)

From this discussion we learn that the IS is an ideal beyond normal human capacity. It is external to any individual and requires a high level of self-control to effectively appropriate it into life's dilemmas, even though nature has made it possible for us to identify with its qualities. It represents a form of telos from which a moral life can be ordered.

However, there are times when public pressure opposes the IS's judgment for a person, and in those instances the influence of the spectator will become weak and faltering, leaving the person with only sympathy to guide action. Smith suggests:

In such cases, this demigod within the breast appears like the demigods of the poets, though partly of immortal, yet partly too of mortal extraction. When his judgements are steadily and firmly directed by the sense of praiseworthiness and blame-worthiness, he seems to act suitably to his divine extraction: But when he suffers himself to be astonished and confounded by the judgements of ignorant and weak man, he discovers his connexion with mortality, and appears to act suitably, rather to the human, than to the divine, part of his origin.

(Smith, TMS, 131)

The All Seeing Judge: A Third Moral Screen of Behavior

This discussion of the divine and human extraction of the IS leaves the possibility of unsolved moral dilemmas when there is no reliable guidance left for a person involved in such a situation. Commenting on the mortal side of the IS, Smith concludes that there are times when the IS is no more dependable than the man without public sympathy who accepts options that are not just or ethical.

In such cases, the only effectual consolation of humbled and afflicted man lies in an appeal to a still higher tribunal, to that of the all-seeing Judge of the world, whose eye can never be deceived, and whose judgments can never be perverted. A firm confidence in the unerring rectitude of this great tribunal, before which his innocence is in due time to be declared, and his virtue to be finally rewarded, can alone support him under the weakness and despondency of his own mind, under the perturbation and astonishment of the man within the breast, whom nature has set up as, in this life, the great guardian, not only of his innocence, but of his tranquility. Our happiness in this life is thus, upon many occasions, dependent upon the humble hope and expectation of a life to come: a hope and expectation deeply rooted in human nature; which can alone support its lofty ideas of its own dignity.

(Smith, *TMS*, 131–132)

Smith believed that the idea of life beyond death, where justice is fully realized, was a valuable contributor to the willingness of individuals to transcend a weak person within and a faulty one without. Having this fully immortal backup to the IS, whether real or imagined, would be the final line of defense against antisocial behavior. Religious values could be beneficial to a social order. In this sense, Smith, though espousing only a natural religion, adopted a concept of telos that specified how people would behave if they lived up to what they were intended to be.

The Stoic tradition, which can be seen beneath the surface of Smith's moral analysis, was influential from early Hellenistic philosophy through the Roman period up to the third century. Fundamental to Stoic thinking was the notion that the world is an ideally good organism that operates as a system with each part serving the whole. A divine *logos,* or primary moving force, ordained the system and acted as its guide. Though later Stoicism developed a more pragmatic, ethical posture, moral development in the Stoic view involved an ever-expanding sense of one's self-interest until the good of the whole is foremost even to the point of sacrificing what would commonly be one's personal interest. The notion of self-control in Stoicism gives clues as to how one progresses morally. Smith's ability to connect the developmental organic qualities of the Stoic view of the world with the mechanistic ordered approach of the eighteenth-century Enlightenment era provided a broad base on which he built his views. The notion of moral progress in Stoicism, when blended with the Enlightenment ideas of moral precepts, led Smith to this three-level approach to the moral socializing of behavior. The ability to exercise sympathy and appropriate the impartial spectator and, if need be, the final judge of our conduct can be seen as a marriage of Stoic moral development and the secular virtue concepts of David Hume. Contemporary attempts to collapse this moral theory back into a modern value-free notion of individualized self-interest seems to be a task almost beyond the

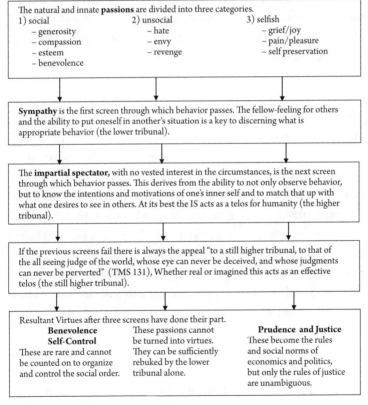

Figure 4.1 Adam Smith's Moral Philosophy

imagination. The notion of an invisible hand, rarely mentioned in Smith's work, does not minimize the role of moral reflection in resource allocation.

Figure 4.1 envisions Smith's moral philosophy. Beginning with the passions inherent in people, the three screens that act to transform the passions into virtues are shown. The social passions are generosity, compassion, and esteem. They are inherently good and bring forth virtuous behavior, but they are also scarce and not prevalent enough in everyday life to serve as the foundation of a successful social order. The unsocial passions of hate, envy, and revenge are so repulsive to humans that they are suppressed in normal cases. The third category of selfish passions includes grief and joy, pain and pleasure, and self-preservation. These have the potential for both good and bad responses, and so a process of socialization and moral conditioning is needed before they can generate virtuous behavior.

Since most of economic life is played out in the area of the selfish passions, the virtues of prudence and justice are of special interest for this study. Does the process of values formation previously described produce the kind of people that can function in an unconstrained economy that is free, open, and productive? Smith believed that if the proper institutional structures were established and new rules of the economic game could be set, then a new era of economic performance would result. The reason for established rules in a social order relates to the problem of appropriating the IS. Since all the circumstances and motivations must be known before the IS can authoritatively speak and because humans rarely know those things in advance, it is necessary to set up general practices and rules that simplify the moral discernment process. Smith states the problem as follows: "So partial are the views of mankind with regard to the propriety of their own conduct, both at the time of action and after it; and so difficult is it for them to view it in the light in which any indifferent spectator would consider it" (Smith, *TMS*,

158). Given this problem and the fact that individuals are easily self-deceived, Smith sees in nature a method that can standardize behavior effectively. We observe behavior that generates individual welfare and social harmony, and we see behavior that does not: "It is thus that general rules of morality are formed. They are ultimately founded upon experience of what, in particular instances, our moral faculties, our natural sense of merit and demerit, approve, or disapprove of" (Smith, *TMS*, 159). Once the rules are established it becomes the duty of everyone to follow the rules. Apparently nature reinforces the opinion that the deity is behind the rules and will subtly enforce them. "Those vicegerents of God within us," Smith asserts, "never fail to punish the violation of them, (rules) by the torments of inward shame, and self-condemnation; and on the contrary, always reward obedience with tranquility of mind, with contentment, and self-satisfaction" (Smith, *TMS*, 166).

Yet for Smith the rules are limited in their purpose. In discussing the operation of virtue development, Smith divides the process into efficient and final causes. The efficient cause of the heart, arteries, and veins is to transport blood. The efficient cause of the wheels of a clock is to spin with consistency. The final cause of the body is to make human life meaningful, and the final cause of the watch is to tell time. At this point, Smith claims that we are trying to do too much if we focus on final causes.

But though, in accounting for the operations of bodies, we never fail to distinguish in this manner the efficient from the final cause, in accounting for those of the mind we are apt to confound these two different things with one another. When by natural principles we are led to advance those ends, which a refined and enlightened reason would recommend to us, we are very apt to impute to that reason, as to their efficient cause, the sentiments and actions by which we advance those ends, and to imagine that to be the wisdom of man, which in reality is the wisdom of God.

(Smith, *TMS*, 87)

This passage illustrates Smith's concern that we confuse natural systems, which function as efficient causes, with the ends of social organization, which are final causes. In this case, Smith argues that the process of transforming the passions into virtues is a natural systemic process, which should be seen as an efficient cause. When a successful social order results, we mistakenly attribute that to our reason rather than to the design of God who alone shaped the final cause.

For some it is a short step from Smith to the spontaneous order of Friedrich Hayek. In regard to the final cause of the social order, Smith is not optimistic that humans can engage in meaningful dialogue. Also, Smith is quite concerned that religious interference with natural principles affects the quality of life for the worse. Yet despite the principles of sympathy, moral approbation, and the IS, which are nature's tools for effective social organization, there is a great degree of ambiguity in life so that some balance must be struck between following nature's prescribed path and feeling one's way along by some dialogical process. Smith raises this concern: "It may be a question, however, in what cases our actions ought to arise chiefly or entirely from a sense of duty, or from a regard to general rules; and in what cases some other sentiment or affection ought to concur, and have a principle influence" (Smith, *TMS*, 171).

This opens the door to great latitude in how the passions relate to general rules or principles in the process of virtue formation. In the previous chart, the passions were divided into three categories. The social passions needed no softening from sympathy and no correction from the IS. They are approved of without any natural general rules in the system. As Smith contends, "All those graceful and admired actions, to which the benevolent affections would prompt us, ought to proceed as much from the passions themselves as from any regard to the general rules of conduct" (Smith, *TMS*, 172).

The unsocial passions require the opposite response. General rules are needed to control these passions and the societal response to those passions because the fact they are socially abhorrent may prompt excessive punishment. However, the selfish passions are open to considerable debate when it comes to their free exercise, the restraint of general rules, or the case-by-case appeal to moral dialogue. All three avenues of expression for the selfish passions are possibilities. "The pursuit of the objects of private interest, in all common little, and ordinary cases, ought to flow rather from a regard to the general rules which prescribe such conduct, than from any passion for the objects themselves; but upon more impor-tant and extraordinary occasions, we should be awkward, insipid, and ungraceful, if the objects themselves did not appear to animate us with a considerable degree of passion" (Smith, *TMS*, 172–173). Misers or those who make much of small gains for themselves let passions control when general rules should restrain the selfish response. A petty self-serving nature cannot be approved, but on larger matters, if one does not pursue one's own interest, any rea-sonable observer rebukes him. After a series of examples showing how a gentleman, a member of parliament, and a tradesman are expected to pursue their interests, Smith observes that ambition, "when it keeps within the bounds of prudence and justice, is always admired in the world, and has even sometimes a certain irregular greatness, which dazzles the imagination, when it passes the lim-its of both these virtues, and is not only unjust but extravagant" (Smith, *TMS*, 173).

Ambition is only one example of how general rules and princi-ples vary and are vague and ambiguous. Smith observes:

The general rules of almost all the virtues, the general rules which determine what are the offices of prudence, of charity, of generosity, of gratitude, of friendship, are in many respects loose and inaccurate, admit of many exceptions, and require so many modifications, that it is scarce possible to regulate our conduct entirely by a regard to them. The common proverbial maxims of prudence, being founded in universal experience, are perhaps the best general rules which can be given about it. To effect, however, a very strict and literal adherence to them would evidently be the most absurd and ridiculous pedantry.

(Smith, *TMS*, 174)

Prudence may prescribe basic rules of order and conduct, but their practical application requires significant dialogue and discernment. Only in the area of justice is Smith clear that rules and rules alone should determine proper action. For Smith, justice is following the commonly accepted rules to which one is committed. Contractual obligations should not be violated, any form of cheating cannot compromise honesty, and slippery slope moral reasoning of any kind will ultimately pervert the system. "The rules of justice may be compared to the rules of grammar; the rules of the other virtues to the rules which critics lay down for the attainment of what is sublime and elegant in composition" (Smith, *TMS*, 175).

Smith's clarity with respect to justice is most evident when he considers exchange in the marketplace. Here Smith expresses his voice as moral philosopher and as "empirical observer and social critic" (Evensky, 2007). As moral philosopher, Smith affirms that self-interest is coupled with the desire for social approval and the approval of the impartial spectator as well as the all-seeing judge of the universe. In Smith's words: "If he would act so as that the impartial spectator may enter into the principles of his conduct, which is what of all things he has the greatest desire to do, he must, upon this, as upon all other occasions, humble the arrogance of his self-love, and bring it down to something which other men can go along with" (Smith, *TMS*, 83). As empirical observer, Smith notes that market interactions represent one familiar place in which the control of self-love is necessary. In commerce we see a tangible example of the phenomenon of passions being transformed into virtues.

Smith's discussion of the evolution of exchange practices is guided by his reflection on the moral bounds that are needed to govern trade. Prior to the agricultural revolution, personal exchange within and among tribes centered on the products gleaned from hunting, gathering, and shepherding. As expanded resource specialization gave rise to the commercial stage, the most advanced state of human progress, impersonal exchange became increasingly prevalent. Smith places particular emphasis on the need for certain moral foundations so that market processes will function well in a commercial society. Thus trust and "honest dealing" are required; restraint of self-love channeled toward winning the favor of others in the civilized commercial society is needed because, with advances in the division of labor, "man has almost constant occasion for the help of his brethren, and it is in vain for him to expect it from their benevolence only" (Smith, *WN*, 26). Rather than depending on the benevolence of others he may or may not know well, "He will be more likely to prevail if he can interest their self-love in his favor, and show them that it is for their own advantage to do for him what he requires of them" (Smith, *WN*, 26). This helps explain how we may engage in mutually advantageous cooperation with individuals we don't know well.

Smith makes it clear that to gain from trade in the impersonal marketplace one cannot depend on "the benevolence of the butcher, the brewer, or the baker" but rather one must appeal "to their self-love" (Smith, *WN*, 27). In doing so, we must restrain our own self-love. Smith's reasoning about the expansion of the division of labor and the evolution of institutional formation from primitive to commercial society suggests that the benevolence found in personal exchanges can be "institutionalized" in the form of impersonal codes in society ordered by market arrangements (Young 1997). Young convincingly shows that "while markets would appear to be impersonal and operating according to their own internal natural laws...nonetheless, the whole process is rooted in institutions which have their origin in the moral sentiments" and moral virtues "such as honesty and trust would actually evolve with the institutions" (Young 1997, 71). The impartial spectator remains present in impersonal exchanges; he or she leads Smith's "man" in the marketplace to qualify his self-interest and, in doing so, contributes to forming a social cohesion that proves effective over time, for it grounds moral behavior in a person's "real interest."

Smith argues that some forms of virtuous behavior become institutionalized through market arrangements. He writes: "Whenever commerce is introduced into any country, probity and punctuality always accompany it" (Smith, *LJ*, 538). Smith goes on to elaborate as to why honesty in exchange and fair dealing are so valued in a commercial society: "Wherever dealings are frequent, a man does not expect to gain so much by any one contract as by probity and punctuality in the whole and a prudent dealer, who is sensible of his real interest, would rather choose to lose what he has a right to than give any ground for suspicion" (Smith, *LJ*, 539). In other words, a merchant will not insist on even his own rights if, by doing so, some credibility will be lost. Self-interest is closely tied to judgments about how one's actions are viewed by others, and the real interest of the merchant is closely tied to the cultivation of a reputation for commendable qualities such as probity and punctuality, qualities modern economists recognize as crucial social norms for the further advancement of market activities. Interestingly, as the British Industrial Revolution was gaining momentum in the latter half of Smith's life, it is also evident that related social norms engendered "cooperation through private-order institutions supporting the progress of useful knowledge and advances of technology" (Mokyr, 369). Smith's writings do not acknowledge the dissemination of technological advance in the late eighteenth century, but they do reflect other contemporary social concerns.

Smith clearly believed markets could manifest human malevolence as well as benevolence. Some of the manifestations of the vices of commercial society he discusses include the practices of prodigal borrowing for speculation in the loanable funds market (Smith, *WN*, 350), combinations of employers and combinations of laborers whose relationships can involve violent clashes (Smith, *WN*, 84–85)[1] and the corruption of moral sentiments by avarice through domination exercised in the enslavement of Africans in the British colonies (Smith, *WN*, 388). In addition, the phenomenon of deceitful practices in the marketplace by laborers, employers, and merchants is perhaps the vice Smith most extensively discusses, as shown in the vignette at the end of this chapter. At the same time, Smith is explicit in contrasting the evident widespread practice of probity in a commercial society with the commonly found lack of honesty practiced by those engaging in social interplay often outside the marketplace in "the superior stations of life." This is where "flattery and falsehood too often prevail over merit and abilities" (Smith, *TMS*, 63).

---

1. For a discussion of Smith's concept of economic justice in the labor market as applied to the relationship between the combinations of employers and laborers respectively, see Noell (1995).

This examination of the process of transforming the passions into virtues leaves many aspects of life, including economic life, open to subjective analysis conditioned by the moral screens. Almost all of the discussion about what makes the selfish passions virtuous involves moral reflection of some kind. Smith describes the complexity of the moral life in great detail. "Before any thing, therefore, can be the complete and proper object, either of gratitude or resentment, it must possess three different qualifications. First, it must be the cause of pleasure in the one case and of pain in the other. Secondly, it must be capable of feeling those sensations. And, thirdly, it must not only have produced those sensations, but it must have produced them from design, and from a design that is approved of in the one case, and disapproved of in the other" (Smith, *TMS*, 96). In other words, the moral life involves effective action from pure motives approved of by sympathy and the impartial spectator.

In the final analysis, for Adam Smith, the path to virtue is filled with moral reflection that involves a dialogue between people as they tend to be and people as they ought to be if they realized their true telos. What Smith rejects is not the notion of a moral reference point outside the person but a coercive duty-bound moral reference point derived from oppressive religion (Halteman, 203). This assertion is decidedly controversial because it implies that morality has its origin in revelation or some force outside human experience. While for Hume this is certainly not true, there is sufficient ambiguity in Smith's work to suggest that the second and third tribunals are not merely based on sympathy and one's ability to impartially judge what is generally deemed appropriate in the social order. What follows in chapter 5 is the story of how economic thinking moved away from Smith's concern with the moral life and became a discipline purported to be value-free in its methodology.

ADAM SMITH AND THE MORAL PREREQUISITE OF MARKETS

Adam Smith is frequently called the "father of economics," and his description of how specialization and trade lead to efficient markets has made *The Wealth of Nations* an enduring classic. The assumptions of perfect competition support a system like the one Smith proposed, but there is one glaring omission in that list. Smith wrote another book to show that economic players must have a moral sense so that a police state will not be necessary to enforce the rules of competition in the market economy. Unfortunately, most economics texts assume, rather than explore, the nature of that moral sense on which a free society is built.

For Smith, ethical behavior is not a cost-benefit calculation but rather the result of an inner emotion or sentiment that compels us to evaluate our behavior in light of the context in which we live and the desire we have to be approved of by others. This desire is so strong that we are able to imagine ourselves in another's shoes observing our behavior and judging it as he or she might. This objectivity becomes a basis for our discernment of what is appropriate for a given time and place. Smith called this imaginative perspective sympathy, and it formed the basis for the moral restraint that is necessary for a free society to function. However, the tension between self-interest and sympathy is sometimes not easily resolved. In such cases, according to Smith, individuals have the capacity to step away from their biases and impartially judge their own behavior. This capacity to become an impartial spectator attuned to a moral sense that is part of us from creation complements sympathy, so that self-control will dominate the unsocial passions that are also part of our makeup and external policing can be minimized. Given this twofold moral defense against our unsocial passions, it becomes possible to exercise free market exchanges with minimal transaction costs and government interference. Thus another assumption of perfect competition is that an effective moral restraint operates by nature in all of us.

Questions for Discussion

1. How much of your behavior is influenced by social opinion?
2. Give examples of how you might step back from your biases and even public opinion to do what seemed to be right. (Think of examples such as Enron's devious corporate mismanagement or unpopular political stands taken by political figures.)
3. If you saw someone drop a $100 bill and you could retrieve it without anyone knowing, what is the moral process that might cause you to return it to the person who lost it?
4. Is Adam Smith correct in suggesting that the social glue of a free society is not only a carefully reasoned cost-benefit analysis but also a form of moral discernment that originates with the emotions and sentiments implanted in us at birth and nurtured by social norms and customs?

ADAM SMITH AND THE PROBLEM OF DECEITFUL CONSPIRACY IN THE MARKETPLACE

As suggested in this chapter on Adam Smith's moral philosophy of economics, Smith employs "two voices" in his writings. One is that of moral philosopher, the other that of an empirical observer of market behavior. When he brings the latter to bear in the *WN*, he does not neglect the distinction he has previously developed between the virtue of probity and the harmfulness of deceit of others. While a commercial society fosters honesty, there remains the reality of deceit as a failure to disclose vital information to others or a misrepresentation of one's true economic condition in the marketplace. Smith recognizes examples in both the product market and the labor market in which we might say that even the powerful forces of self-command, conscience, and the impartial spectator do not foster the virtue of honesty.

Consider first what he says about instances of suppliers determining to withhold information from rival suppliers so as to limit competition. They do so in order to continue benefiting from the market price being kept artificially above the natural price:

> When by an increase in the effectual demand, the market price of some commodity happens to rise a great deal above the natural price, those who employ their stocks in supplying that market are generally careful to conceal this change. If it was commonly known, their great profit would tempt so many new rivals to employ their stocks in the same way, that, the effectual demand being fully supplied, the market price would soon be reduced to the natural price, and perhaps for some time even below it.
>
> (Smith, *WN*, 77)

In this instance, the deceitful conspiracy involves only a portion of the suppliers of a given product. Here the purpose of deceit is to "prevent natural outcomes from occurring" (Brown, 82).

Such behavior of a "man of reserve and concealment" is also exhibited by an employer who, as part of the wage-bargaining process, conspires with fellow employers to suppress wages (Smith, *TMS*, 29). Employers enter into combinations in order to lower the wages of laborers, efforts " conducted with the utmost silence and secrecy, till the moment of execution" when the laborers yield to accepting a lower wage (Smith, *WN*, 84). The masters secretly collude to reduce their payroll costs yet vocally proclaim their need for the assistance of the law. In the second half of the eighteenth century, the British law is bent in favor of employers and against the efforts of laborers to combine as a countervailing force to prop up their wages (Smith, *WN*, 157–158).

In an oft-quoted statement, Smith captures the tendency for rivals on the same "side of the market" to succumb to the temptation to secretly end their competition and benefit; thereby "[P]eople of the same trade seldom meet together, even for merriment and diversion, but the conversation ends in a conspiracy against the public, or in some contrivance to raise prices" (Smith, *WN*, 145). Today advocates of the vigorous antitrust prosecution of "conspiracies to restrain trade" in both the United States and Europe often cite Smith's statement in support of their efforts. Recognition of such a tendency has even fostered antitrust prosecution against price-fixing conspiracies in a diverse range of industries, including electrical equipment, vitamins, and petroleum. Yet Smith's further observation is often overlooked by policymakers: "It is impossible indeed to prevent such meetings, by any law which either could be executed, or would be consistent with liberty and justice. But though the law cannot hinder people of the same trade from sometimes assembling together, it ought to do nothing to facilitate such assemblies; much less to render them necessary" (Smith, *WN*, 145). A careful look at the context of Smith's discussion of deceitful conspiracies in book 1, chapter 10 of the *WN* shows that Smith wants the law to be impartial, not encouraging nor prohibiting combinations on either side of the labor market (Noell 1995).

In neither of these two cases of deceit does Smith appeal to the need for legislative intervention. He disputes instead the ability of governmental authorities to act in a manner consistent with justice to correct these cases of abuse by market combinations. As Coase suggests, Smith would be concerned that, even if a government official is motivated by benevolence in implementing regulation, he "will tend to favor his family, his friends, members of his party, [and/or] inhabitants of his region or country (and this whether or not he is democratically elected)" (Coase, 544). Instead Smith would presumably prefer that self-regulating social forces be given the opportunity to overcome deceitful commercial practices.

Questions for Discussion

1. What recent examples come to mind of reported conspiratorial behavior by firms acting as either producers or employers?
2. Does Smith provide a convincing rationale for government inaction against market combinations? Why or why not?
3. Will justice always require impartiality of the law to combinations of groups on either side of the product or labor market? Explain.
4. Can antitrust laws be successfully designed and enforced and still not violate economic liberty? Explain.

Chapter 5

The Secularization of Political Economy

The path from the concerns of Adam Smith to those of the modern economist is circuitous. What has not been emphasized in the previous chapter is the political economy of Smith as depicted in *An Inquiry into the Nature and Causes of the Wealth of Nations* (*WN*). If that book is read within the context of Smith's moral theory, it will seem a much different work than if a reader considers the *WN* alone. Smith is concerned with the governmental management of the economy that characterized the mercantilist view of political economy. The notion that wealth consisted of hoards of precious metals led to many practices that constrained rather than stimulated economic activity. A perpetual positive balance of trade, imperialistic expansion of power over distant colonies, high tax rates, and an assortment of regulations and fees could, for a time, bolster a national treasury. The fragmentation of feudal society stimulated a search for security in a stronger nation-state, but Smith saw beyond the short-term concerns to the longer-term prospect of universal opulence in a free economy. He saw a process of growth and development based on specialization and trade. He explored the notion that certain principles of nature, given the right institutional environment, could lead to social harmony even as individuals pursued their own interests. But all of this was contingent on the belief that individuals acted within the bounds of moral sentiments, which meant that sympathy and the impartial spectator were operative. Smith's view that all value originated in labor put human welfare at the center of his system for progress. It is strange that Smith never mentioned the role of moral sentiments in the *WN*, but it is clear that he maintained his sensitivity to human values throughout that economic treatise.

What is clear is that Smith saw economic life as a social process needing care and adjustment. His concern for government intervention did not make him an enemy of government but rather a vigilant protector of free exchange as a system. Competition was a dynamic process that compelled economic agents to perform at their best. Compared with the end-state equilibriums of modern welfare economics, Smith would fit better with the institutionalists in terms of method, historical awareness, and interdisciplinary facility. According to Marc Blaug, "the effort in modern textbooks to enlist Adam Smith in support of what is now known as the 'fundamental theorems of welfare economics'…is a historical travesty of major proportions" (Blaug, 60).

For Smith, economics was embedded in the historical, psychological, and social fabric of society where moral reflection was natural and important. As classical economics moved into the nineteenth century, moral reflection became personal at best and counterproductive at worst. From 1800 to approximately 1850, a group of influential writers built on the work of David Hume, Smith, and the natural law philosophers to construct an economic system that was embedded in nature and to which human law needed to conform. D. P. O'Brien lists four propositions that are foundational to this classical economic thinking: "[t]hat there is an underlying order in material phenomena; that this underlying order is discoverable either by reasoning from observed phenomena or from innate moral sense; that discovery of the underlying order leads to the formulation of natural laws which, if followed, lead to the best possible situation; and that positive legislation should reflect these natural laws" (O'Brien, 27).

For Adam Smith the innate moral sense was important to all behavior, and it originated, not in cognitive reasoning, but in the senses and the imagination. It is possible to see in Smith's work traces of Aristotle's metaphysical biology with its focus on what is natural. The natural law tradition of Thomas Aquinas and other scholastics also pointed to principles in creation that could direct humans to a fulfilling life. According to O'Brien, this "optimistic teleology" with its source in God became secularized in the late Middle Ages by Protestant theorists such as Hugo Grotius, Samuel von Pufendorf, and Francis Hutcheson (O'Brien, 28). This secularization process was helped along by the rigidity and exclusiveness of Christendom, which led the state to imprison, execute, or expel thinkers who professed ideas that ran counter to those of the established church. Thinkers like Grotius and Pufendorf objected to various religious doctrines and behavioral regulations seeking rather to find natural laws that would proscribe human behavior. While this secularization opened the door for eventual deistic views of the way the world works, it did not necessarily lead to the loss of telos in moral thinking. As was argued in the last chapter, Smith retained the need for moral reflection in a social order that could not be reduced completely to naturalistic thinking. However, for his successors, David Ricardo, Thomas Malthus, J. B. Say, John Stuart Mill, Jeremy Bentham, and others, the search for the ideal system began to focus increasingly on a methodology similar to that of classical physics. The political economy agenda became the rational discovery of the underlying principles of society and the fitting of human law to those principles. Increasingly seduced by the methods of classical physics and the desire to be a respectable science, economics eventually adopted a methodology with value-free scientific tools and a primary goal of prediction. Yet the secularization of political economy took almost a hundred years and it is instructive to examine some of the steps taken by the classical economists along the way. What follows is a brief sketch of this drift from reasoning with a moral sense to reasoning exclusively from observable phenomena.

The purpose here is not to explore all the economic theories and controversies for which Malthus, Ricardo, and other classical economists are famous. Rather it is to look at the methods they used and consider how those methods impacted moral reflection in economic conversation. When much of the rhetoric is stripped away, methodological discussion frequently centers on the degree to which intentional human action can alter particular circumstances. In the preface to *Principles of Political Economy and Taxation,* Ricardo clearly states his belief in naturalism as the driving force of economic life, and he is critical of other classical writers who were willing to afford a role for a more subjective, less deterministic methodology. Speaking of the theory of the distribution of income among landowners, labor, and capital owners, Ricardo claims that "[T]o determine the laws which regulate this distribution is the principal problem of Political Economy: much as the science has been improved by Turgot, Stuart, Smith, Say, Sismondi, and others, they afford very little satisfactory information respecting the natural course of rent, profit, and wages" (Ricardo, 1). If we are subject to immutable laws of social organization that will have their way in time irrespective of our policy efforts, then the best strategy is to uncover those laws or principles and establish social institutions that submit to them with the least intrusion on the way the system functions. Because such a strategy would be consistent with nature and would involve less costly and useless interventions, it can be argued that a laissez-faire bias in political economy would be morally preferable. If the resource provisioning process is a natural system, it is possible to see its relationships as mechanical and amenable to mathematical analysis. Thus, political economy became economics with deductive rationality, mathematics, and a positive-normative dichotomy shaping its methodology. Progress and economic growth would be sufficient moral justification for the system.

Ricardo led the way in conceptualizing the economy as a system determined by nature. His clarification of the quantity theory of money, his insights into the diminishing returns in production and its impact on rent, and his illumination of the theory of comparative advantage in trade relations all solidified the notion that economic forces were connected in a system that would have its way without intervention from policy makers or moralists.

In Europe, concerns about income distribution and rising poverty dominated the period from 1725 to 1825. Despite the increased production hastened by the Industrial Revolution, the standard of living for laborers declined, as measured by the ratio of income divided by the cost of a day laborer's basket of consumer goods. It was difficult for an average-sized family of the laborer to maintain the standard of living that had prevailed three hundred years before (Allen, 39). It is interesting that housing was measured as only 5 percent of a subsistence consumer basket indicating that rental conditions in the cities were deplorable in many cases (Allen, 38). In contrast to what many of his contemporaries believed, Ricardo saw this poverty as inevitable because of natural human reproductive tendencies:

> It is when the market price of labour exceeds its natural price that the condition of the labourer is flourishing and happy, that he has it in his power to command a greater proportion of the necessaries and enjoyments of life, and therefore to rear a healthy and numerous family. When however, by the

encouragement which high wages give to the increase of population, the number of labourers is increased, wages again fall to
their natural price, and indeed from a reaction sometimes fall
below it.

(Ricardo, 45–46)

In this view, Ricardo was following Malthus, whose focus on
population trends led him to be skeptical of intentional efforts to
solve the poverty problem. Thomas Malthus begins his essay with
the stated purpose "[T]o investigate the causes that have hitherto
impeded the progress of mankind towards happiness" (Malthus,
1). His assumption from the beginning about poverty and hardship
was that there was "one great cause intimately united with the very
nature of man; which, though it has been constantly and power-
fully operating since the commencement of society, has been little
noticed by the writers who have treated this subject" (Malthus, 1).
In Malthus's first edition of *An Essay on the Principle of Population,*
he focused on the inevitability of the positive checks of pestilence
and famine that kept population in balance with food supply as
if nature was the cause and solution to excessive population and
therefore poverty.

For both Ricardo and Malthus, the phrases *natural price* and
nature of man tended to soften any moral obligation to help the poor,
because the system of supply and demand coupled with the "law of
population growth" would mean poverty was here to stay. Nature
ultimately determined labor's position in life, and the efforts of
moralists to improve on nature's work would be futile.

Mill, who also accepted Malthus's dismal population predictions as likely, felt that it might be possible for rational moral
reflection to overcome the iron law of subsistence wages. Rudi
Verberg makes a case for Mill as one classical economist unwilling
to divorce moral reflection from economics. By examining Mill's

political, economic, and moral ideas as a whole, Verberg concludes that Mill saw the possibility of moral progress as people became better educated on the issues involved. Moral reflection, enlightened self-interest, and interest in the common good, can all evolve from within the system as freedom and progress work together for the betterment of society. Verberg quotes from Mill's autobiography to illustrate Mill's optimism: "Interest in the common good is at present so weak a motive in the generality, not because it can never be otherwise, but because the mind is not accustomed to dwell on it as it dwells from morning till night on things which tend only to personal advantage" (Verberg, 235). According to Verberg, Mill worked to show the linkages between political economy as a science and political economy as an art, but because classical economics was becoming increasingly rational and scientific, the possibility for moral reflection that Mill envisioned was eventually lost.

While Ricardo, Malthus, and Mill focused on the production side of economic life to show how nature's production principles influenced resource allocation, Jeremy Bentham was observing that the demand side of the market was also structured by nature and therefore not in need of moral reflection as a dialogical process. For Bentham, the foundation of ethical norms was not derived from a source outside creation. Instead, the experience of pain and pleasure became the metric for morality. Bentham's comments cited in chapter 1 makes this point vivid:

> Nature has placed mankind under the governance of two sovereign masters, pain and pleasure. It is for them alone to point out what we ought to do, as well as to determine what we shall do. On the one hand the standard of right and wrong, on the other the chain of causes and effects, are fastened to their throne. They govern us in all we do, in all we say, in all we think: every

effort we can make to throw off our subjection, will serve but to demonstrate and confirm it.

(Bentham, 166)

Moral reflection, in this view, is nothing more than the calibration of personal feelings and the optimization of net pleasure. The feelings are determined by nature rather than subjective contemplation. We are governed by and subject to nature, rather than being moral agents responsible for discerning what is right and good.

Building on this framework, in 1860 William Stanley Jevons applied this thinking to shift the source of value in economic analysis from objective cost measured by labor effort to subjective utility measured by individual preferences as expressed in the demand for goods and services. The 1860s were a watershed period in economic thought as several writers independently argued that the value of a good or service depended on the pleasure gained from the last unit consumed by the consumer. Some frivolous trinket that took little time and few resources to produce could sell for a high price as long as it caught the fancy of consumers. While the cost of production still conditioned how many items would be produced, the exchange value was still determined by the marginal utility realized in a competitive market. That value originated from the natural principle of diminishing marginal utility in consumption rather than from any moral reflection. To Jevons, labor value was determined by a product's price rather than price being determined by the cost of labor expended in production. As he states, "I hold labour to be essentially variable, so that its value must be determined by the value of the produce, not the value of the produce by that of the labour" (Jevons, 410). When coupled with the Ricardian production side of the market, this utilitarian view of the demand side of the market puts the entire market outside the bounds of moral reflection and practical ethics.

Reflecting on the outcomes of classical economic thinking, John Maynard Keynes found the dominance of the Ricardian system a curious and mysterious reality. He attributed it to the fact that it met a need of the times, that its counterintuitive findings added intellectual attraction, that its broad scope gave it beauty, and that it promoted freedom for capitalists to pursue their wishes. In regard to the way it provided an escape from moral accountability, Keynes declared "[T]hat it could explain much social injustice and apparent cruelty as an inevitable incident in the scheme of progress, and the attempt to change such things as likely on the whole to do more harm than good, commended its authority" (Keynes 1965, 33).

By quantifying production functions and utility functions, the process of optimizing the system into a general equilibrium framework was undertaken by what we now call the neoclassical economists. This quantifiable structured system became a model for how the world worked economically, and moral considerations were eliminated from the process. The metamorphosis of political economy to economics was now nearing its completion. Economics could generate predictions and it fit more closely with mathematics and the physical sciences. One mathematician who qualified this trend was Alfred Marshall. While his name is most closely associated with neoclassical economics and his *Principles of Economics* book of 1890 became the standard text of the discipline for at least forty years, Marshall was uneasy about the divorce between economics and moral reflection. While he did much to solidify neoclassical market theory, he did not promote economics as a value-free enterprise. He voiced his concern about the demise of moral and ethical thinking in economics as follows: "But ethical forces are among those of which the economist has to take account. Attempts have indeed been made to construct an abstract science with regard to the actions of an 'economic man' who is under no ethical influences and who pursues pecuniary gain warily and energetically, but mechanically and self-ishly. But they have not been successful, nor even thoroughly carried out" (Marshall 1920, vi). Marshall proceeds to describe people as complex beings with a multitude of motivations and emotions, all of which should not be ignored in economic thinking. In a lecture in 1885, Marshall describes the change that took place from the classi-cal to the neoclassical period:

> The chief fault in English economists at the beginning of the century was not that they ignored history and statistics, but that they regarded man as so to speak a constant quantity, and gave themselves little trouble to study his variations. They therefore attributed to the forces of supply and demand a much more mechanical and regular action than they actually have. Their most vital fault was that they did not see how liable to change are the habits and institutions of industry.
>
> (Marshall, Inaugural Lecture 1885, 155)

In Marshall's *Principles of Economics*, he defines *economics* as "a study of mankind in the ordinary business of life; it examines that part of individual and social action which is most closely connected with the attainment and with the use of the material requisites of wellbe-ing" (Marshall 1920, 1). It is significant that Marshall includes indi-vidual and social action in his definition, and it is also clear that he sees the study of individual behavior as considerably more complex than the simple *homo economicus* models of neoclassical analysis.

Despite Marshall's concerns about a socially sterile discipline, his work became the foundation of a highly mathematical approach to theorizing about economic affairs. The more formal the disci-pline became the more it isolated itself from moral reflection and ethics. By 1906 the French economist Vilfredo Pareto declares that

"[T]he main object of our study is economic equilibrium" (Pareto, 477). When he later defines *equilibrium*, it is clear that the process of adjustment is not in the picture:

> It can be said that economic equilibrium is that state which maintains itself indefinitely if there is no change in the conditions which are being studied. If for the moment we direct our attention only to the stable equilibrium, we can say that it is determined in such a fashion that if it is only slightly modified, it immediately tends to right itself—to return to its previous state....It will be necessary to explain mathematically that once this equilibrium has been attained, these variations, or, if you like, these movements, will not occur; which brings us back to the statement that the system maintains itself indefinitely in the state under consideration.
>
> (Pareto 479)

Economics increasingly began to move toward being a study of equilibrium states and away from the scrutinizing of processes of adjustment, alternative human motivations, and moral reflection. For many, this seemed like emancipation from religion and its moralistic teachings and a welcome shift toward science with its more definitive findings. With systemic automatic adjustments there was little room left for subjective input of any kind, and moral reflection hardly lent itself to equilibrium models.

The motivation behind this trend centered on the notion that ideology and belief muddied the waters of analysis. The realities of the early twentieth century convinced many that the "isms" of the world, when connected with economic systems, led to disaster. Fascism and communism were visions of the world that blended political ideology with economics in ways that were destructive. The moral fervor of these systems coupled with their

obvious failures put moral reflection on social matters in a bad
light:

> The atrocities occurring within totalitarian systems created
> widespread disillusionment with all collectivist schemes, so
> increasing numbers of economists rejected the use of econom-
> ics as a tool for fashioning activist public policies aimed at
> improving society. Intent on keeping ideology out of scientific
> research and analysis, these economists were attracted to a phi-
> losophy called logical positivism developed in Vienna during
> the 1920's. This approach is based on the notion of a clear dis-
> tinction between is and ought, between fact and value, between
> description and prescription.
>
> (Clark, 310)

The early positivists rejected all metaphysical thinking as unscientific because it could not be verified empirically. Only observable
phenomena could be considered scientific truth.

This concept of truth was not only applicable to natural science,
it was a universal method that should be applied to all truth seeking. With such a rigid standard for truth, any moral reflection, metaphysical assertion, or religious claim was dismissed as irrelevant in
the search for truth. Without empirical verification, there is no truth
because scientific verification and truth are synonymous. Bruce
Caldwell, commenting on the positivist truth standards, notes
that "the social sciences no less than the natural sciences are concerned with observable phenomena: thus approaches to the social
disciplines which rely on such devices as, say subconscious motivations or introspective states of mind for the explanation of social
phenomena can be accused of metaphysical speculation" (Caldwell,
16). Over time the rigid standards for scientific inquiry established
by the early positivists were altered somewhat by thinkers such as

Karl Popper, Imre Lakatos, and Thomas Kuhn. Instead of requiring absolute verifiability, Popper argued that a statement must only be falsifiable to be considered scientific, and thus a truth claim that could be falsified but had not been exhaustively tested could be considered scientific. Truth claims could now stand in various stages of confirmation rather than being dismissed as not completely verified.

More than other social sciences, economics accepted the general framework of the positivists, which complemented the trends already present in economic methodology, and the fact-value distinction became firmly embedded in economic textbooks as the twentieth century progressed. Now textbooks on the principles of economics highlight the discipline as having a positive scientific component and a normative speculative component about which no definitive statements can be made. Thus moral reflection is excluded from economics proper, because positive economic science is what economists pursue and normative economics is what policy makers do with economic theory once it is established. The notion that economists can identify how the world will work, given various circumstances and policies, without infusing ideology into their work is still the ruling methodology in the discipline. Rational choice is the analytical device that economists use to develop the generalizations out of which economic theory is formed. This methodology did not go unchallenged from its beginning. The next chapter examines several heterodox critiques of the mainstream, and chapter 7 will take up the task of exploring the strengths and weaknesses of rational choice. Before it can be critiqued it must be understood in terms of its assumptions, its purpose, and its success as a tool. That task will be taken up in chapter 7, after which chapter 8 will explore the more recent frontiers of economics that open doors to increased moral reflection. The final chapter of the book will examine possible ways in which moral reflection can be better integrated into economic thinking.

ALFRED MARSHALL AND THE VALUE OF SOMETHING

"My house is worth only half of what it was last year." "I work as hard as my neighbor, but he gets twice the pay I get." "My General Motors stock just went from $4 to $6 after dropping from $11 to $4." Comments like these were common during 2008 and 2009. Many began to wonder what the value of a given commodity really was. How can things change so fast, and is there no intrinsic value that one can depend on? These questions are not new. In the views of the early classical school of economics, value was measured by how much labor went into the production of a good or service. Over time a house would not change in value even if one might have to lower the price if the sale had to be finalized in a short time. A labor theory of value seemed to work in the long run, and intrinsic value measured in that way made sense to most. Production costs were objective and something the mind can easily grasp and quantify.

However many transactions are made without the benefit of the long-run perspective, and what about the house, the differing wages, and the General Motors (GM) stock? Jeremy Bentham had an answer to that question. The house is worth only what someone is willing to pay for it today, and that will depend on how much pleasure or utility the owner derives from its use. The house has no intrinsic value on its own apart from the value acquired in its use. Wages depend not only on what one produces but also on how much someone wants what is produced. Stock is worthless if the possessor thinks it will return nothing. Value now is related only to the subjective feelings and speculations of those who might purchase what others have to offer. This realization helps the consumer understand why the prices of things can change so fast.

This confusion over value and price was debated by many, but it was Alfred Marshall who finally made sense of the connection between intrinsic and subjective value. They are interdependent with subjective utility forming a demand curve where more is demanded as price falls. Intrinsic value forms a supply curve where more can be supplied as price rises. "We might as reasonably dispute whether it is the upper or the under blade of a pair of scissors that cuts a piece of paper, as whether value is governed by utility or cost of production" (Marshall 1920, 348). Both work together in what is now taught in every principles of economics class as simple supply-and-demand pricing. Yet time is a factor in price determination. "Thus we may conclude that, as a general rule, the shorter the period which we are considering, the greater must be the share of our attention which is given to the influence of demand on value; and the longer the period, the more important will be the influence of cost of production on value" (Marshall 1920, 349).

Marshall, in his 1890 work, *Principles of Economics,* gives us perspective on the questions that we ask today. The price of a house declines because people are fearful of losing their jobs and defaulting on their payments. The pleasure the house will bring them is decreased because of those concerns. My pay is less than my neighbor's because people get more utility from what he produces than from what I produce, and stock prices fluctuate as people speculate on the future of GM. Supply and demand determine price and, of the two, demand is most infused with the values people hold and the moral perspective that is important to them.

Questions for Discussion

1. How can you relate the theory of price to the principles of diminishing marginal utility and decreasing returns to production?
2. Give examples of how one's moral and ethical principles relate to the price of goods and services.
3. Illustrate how the short run and long run make a difference in how a farmer relates to markets.
4. In a short paragraph describe the differences in explaining price among the early classical economists, the utilitarian followers of Jeremy Bentham, and Alfred Marshall.

JOHN STUART MILL: THE LIFE OF *HOMO ECONOMICUS* IS DEPRESSING AT BEST

If you are bright and have felt pushed by a parent to succeed, if you have ever felt overwhelmed and depressed by the mechanical complexity of life, or if the analytical side of life seems to dominate the moral and spiritual concerns you have, then John Stuart Mill is someone to read. From the age of three he was pushed by his father to study Greek and all the disciplines of the liberal arts. By sixteen, he took a job with the East India Company, but his austere childhood that he claims was driven by fear rather than love led to depression and an emotional crisis. With the help of a close friend, however, through poetry and attention to his emotions and moral feelings, Mill was able to become a leading contributor to philosophy, political theory, and economics for nearly half a century. His book on political economy became the primary text for the study of economics throughout the last half of the nineteenth century.

Writing in a time when political economy was searching for the natural laws that governed all aspects of resource production and allocation, Mill challenged the view that there were laws in nature that determined both the way in which production could best be accomplished and the way that output would be allocated among competing interests.

Mill writes, "The laws and conditions of Production of wealth partake of the character of physical truths. There is nothing optional or arbitrary in them.... It is not so with the Distribution of wealth. That is a matter of human institution solely.... The distribution of wealth, therefore, depends on the laws and customs of society" (Mill II.I.I). This claim seemed almost socialist to some, especially after Karl Marx began taking up the cause of workers, but Mill's treatment of wage determination was far less confrontational. He claimed that a competitive market wage was to be the main determining factor in labor's share of production, but when that wage violated social perceptions of justice and fairness, adjustments could be made. "Wages, like other things, may be regulated either by competition or by custom.... Competition, however, must be regarded, in the present state of society, as the principal regulator of wages, and custom or individual character only as a modifying circumstance, and that in a comparatively slight degree" (Mill, II.II.2). This opens the door for what we call today a mixed economy. Markets are the primary allocating mechanism for output, but social norms and moral concerns are always present to temper and adjust market outcomes if the values of society are not achieved by the market. For Mill, this was a liberating concept because it allowed for the emotive and spiritual side of a person to count in the social order. Values and beliefs could become a part of the social framework, and public deliberation and debate on such matters was essential to the flourishing life. The mechanical mathematical utility maximizing *homo economicus* was not a good representation of how the economy would ideally operate, and no one would want to live in a world dominated by mechanistically determined people. Economics is systematic and scientific as well as social and moral.

Questions to Consider

1. Market competition supposedly provides wages equal to what a worker generates in value to the economy. What values or beliefs might alter that distribution pattern?

2. Do you feel like you are merely a cog in an economic machine, or do you feel your place in the system is meaningful and fulfilling?

3. When Mill speaks of "the laws and customs of society" as being helpful in income distribution, presumably some level of government would have to be involved. In what ways can the government implement improvements in income distribution?

4. Is this qualification of *homo economicus* liberating for you as it was for Mill?

Chapter 6

Heterodox Economics and the Varied Manner of Moral Reflection

With the creation of economics as a distinct discipline came the rise of neoclassical economics. This metamorphosis of political economy, accompanied by the adoption of a formalized methodology grounded in rational choice, in turn led to challenges offered by heterodox economics. We explore some of the main themes of the heterodox alternatives by observing the methods employed and the moral themes pursued in the work of three economists, Karl Marx, Thorstein Veblen, and Friedrich Hayek.

Each economist offers a different explanation of the driving forces behind the economic behavior of capitalism. This produces distinctive sets of moral reflections. Yet each approach emphasizes the need to understand the process of change in market-based economies. Moreover, each economist's moral reflections on human nature and/or behavior, the methods of production, and desirable social and economic policy are set against the backdrop of technological innovation and developments in philosophical reasoning. Marx's thought is best understood as a response to the Industrial Revolution as well as certain dimensions of European Enlightenment philosophy. Veblen's economic thought is shaped by the second Industrial Revolution and consequent material gains in the United States, and his methodology draws from the well of

German historicism. Hayek's writings reflect on the advance of what is called scientism and present a detailed case for decentralized market processes even as collectivist economic planning was being adopted by mid-twentieth-century governments.

Karl Marx

Karl Marx, born in nineteenth-century Prussia, is a complex figure in the history of Western thought. He is significant for his contributions as a sociologist, a philosopher, and a historian, as well as for his contributions in economics and for the widespread influence of his ideas. For several decades in the mid-twentieth century, Marx's understanding of the exploitative nature of capitalism and the desirability of implementing socialism was the framework for those who governed more than half of the world's population. Ironically, as a nineteenth-century figure, Marx obviously never experienced firsthand the benefits of this influence but instead resided in exile in London, having been expelled by the governments of Prussia, Belgium, and France. From 1849 onward, Marx lived a life of mere subsistence that was also hampered by periodic illnesses. This did not seem to slow his drive to write and organize, however.

Marx was deeply familiar with the writings of Adam Smith and David Ricardo. He shared their interests in the pursuit of identifying and explaining certain regularities or patterns of economic life. Marx adopted the Enlightenment perspective that there are social laws of motion that the economist can discern and use to forecast change in economic activity. He posited "laws of capitalist motion" that guide the social system. Marx's method was more organic than the mechanical reasoning of Enlightenment figures such as Isaac Newton, but he shared with other Enlightenment-era economists a passion for exploring the nature of capitalism. The "scientific socialism" espoused by Marx and his collaborator, Friedrich Engels, was to be distinguished from other nineteenth-century socialist critiques of capitalism. Struik elaborates on the difference: "Where most socialists merely indicted capitalist society, these two felt the need to understand the mechanism. Where most socialists only stressed the desirability of a new world order, Marx and Engels sought the dynamics by which the change could be performed" (Struik, 35). Marx's moral reflections on capitalism engage not only the direction in which history is headed but the desirability of what he thought was the inevitable downfall of capitalism.

Here the influence on Marx of the German Enlightenment philosopher Georg Hegel's theory of progress in history is evident. History is an organic process guided by the human spirit. Hegel's dialectic posited a process of opposing forces in which a thesis gives rise to antithesis, resulting in a synthesis. Guided by Ludwig Feuerbach's doctrine of materialism, Marx developed historical materialism, his own theory of economic history grounded in the notion that the material world fundamentally shapes our moral and social ideas. No ultimate reality exists beyond the material world. Historical materialism employs dialectical reasoning to explain how production methods and the ownership of capital direct historical change.

For Marx, what moves history is the reality of class struggle engendered by changing modes of production. Prior to the emergence of the capitalist mode of production, this struggle was manifested in the immoral exploitation by masters of slaves, patricians of plebeians, and lords of serfs. Even as human ingenuity finds ever more productive methods to generate output beyond subsistence living, class struggle intensifies between the bourgeois owners of capital and the labor they employ, the proletariat.

By the mid-nineteenth century, capitalism had significantly increased Great Britain's productive capacity. Western Europe was experiencing similar advances as the technological innovations of the Industrial Revolution were applied to manufacturing a variety of consumer and industrial products. In *The Communist Manifesto*, published in 1848, Marx and Engels paid tribute to the immense productive capabilities of capitalism:

> The bourgeoisie during its rule of scarce one hundred years has created more massive and colossal productive forces than have all preceding generations together. Subjection of nature's forces to man, machinery, application of chemistry to industry and agriculture, steam navigation, railways, electric telegraphs, clearing of whole continents for cultivation, canalization of rivers, whole populations conjured out of the ground—what earlier century had even a presentiment that such productive powers slumbered in the lap of social labor?
>
> (Marx and Engels *TCM*, 94)

Yet Marx castigated the bourgeois factory and resource owners for refusing to share the benefits of these productive forces with the workers.

Capitalism is grounded in the private ownership of the means of production. and monetary exchange is an economic system oriented to generate profits for those who own those means of production. Yet humans in Marx's view are "species-beings" meant to participate in both labor and leisure in community-based economic relationships without being driven by the endless pursuit of material gains (what Marx termed "the fetishism of commodities" that existed under capitalism). Marx held that capitalism causes productive activity to become intrinsically soul destroying, for in the pursuit of minimizing costs capitalists adopt production methods that "impoverish the character of work" (Conway, 36–37). In particular, Marx singles out the division of labor, or job specialization, and the mechanization of industry to be exploitative in separating the worker from the product. Marx expands on the deleterious consequences of the capitalist mode of production for laborers:

> Within the capitalist system of production all methods for raising the social productivity of labor are put into effect at the cost of the individual worker; all the means for the development of production...become means of domination...of the producers; they distort the worker into a fragment of a man, they degrade him to the level of an appendage of a machine, they destroy the actual content of his labor by turning it into torment; they alienate from him the intellectual potentialities of the labor process in the same proportion as science is incorporated in it as independent power; they deform the condition under which he works.
>
> (Marx, *Capital*, 799)

Marx also critiques the selfishness that drives individual behavior in capitalist exchange relationships. The bourgeois capitalist regards others as merely a means to an end and is not concerned with the well-being of society. Capitalism fashions a community that doesn't reflect man as a 'species-being.' Indeed, since it is founded upon exchange between self-seeking individuals, it cannot be a true community. Marx affirms that capitalist society, with the backing of the Christian religion, will "sever all the species-bonds of man, establish egoism and selfish need in their place, and dissolve the human world into a world of atomistic, antagonistic individuals" (Marx, [EW], 38-39).

Marx's laws of capitalist motion depicted the dynamics of capitalism in terms of oversupply and disequilibrium. Capitalist economies would lurch from recession to other recessions of increasing magnitude and length. Firms as a whole would overproduce as they added capital, leading to acquisitions of failed firms by larger firms and the concentration of capital. Capitalists would drive more workers into the "reserve army of the unemployed" as they faced excess industrial capacity. Meanwhile the proletariat would grow in its class consciousness as capitalist exploitation heightened. Factory owners would impose poorer working conditions, longer working hours, and lower wages as they faced increasingly severe economic crises. As exploitation increased, workers would recognize the reality of the class struggle. When class consciousness spread among the proletariat sufficiently, its members would arise and overthrow the capitalist economic system, taking the means of production for themselves in a socialist "dictatorship of the proletariat."

Eventually it would be clear there would be no need for private property nor for the state to govern human relations, and communism would be ushered in as the final stage of human history. Marx held that communism is "that form of human association alone adequate to man's nature as a species-being" (Conway, 27). Why did Marx believe that communism was a superior form of societal organization to capitalism? While Marx affirmed that communism could better supply individuals with the goods and services they desired, this was not why the system was superior; rather it was that "communism produces as members of society human beings possessed of better wants and superior accomplishments than capitalism does" (Conway, 29). Thus, Marx finds that "Communist man and woman are far less acquisitive and selfish than their capitalist counterparts. They are thus more altruistic and cooperative. They are reckoned to be more aesthetically sensitive as well as more versatile and creative" (Conway, 29).

Humans are meant to engage with one another freely in community without the shackles of private property and monetary exchange. Marx's valuation of human autonomy drives his moral critique of capitalism. Capitalism presents significant obstacles to the achievement of human autonomy, barriers removed under communist central planning. Marx argues, "With the communistic regulation of production (and implicit in this, the abolition of the alien attitude...of men to their own product), the power of the relation of supply and demand is dissolved into nothing, and men once again gain control of exchange, production, and the way they behave to one another..." (Marx, CW, 48). In the absence of market forces, individuals are free to produce what is needed for society's subsistence without being obliged to engage in any activity outside their own choice. Marx's moral reflection leads him to human autonomy as the telos of engaging in economic activity.

Marx elevated the need for socialist revolution as his highest priority, for only through it would communism be ultimately achieved. In his view, human nature only fully realizes its ultimate purpose in the communist state. In the meantime, Marx and other revolutionaries would push for the overthrow of the capitalist production apparatus and governments that reinforced bourgeois values. They were confident this was an inexorable process that would finally result in the restoration of human nature through a change of institutions, the creation of a "new man" free of a self-centered exploitative bent. This would result in the realization of the telos of social actions, the purpose of human endeavor fulfilled in a society absent of private property and exploitation.

Marx's collaborator, Engels, was convinced that Marx had fashioned a "scientific socialism" that was superior to the romantic, sentimental utopian socialism offered by his peers in the mid-nineteenth century. Marx does not speak of a moral obligation to help the poor; rather he describes the process of economic exploitation of one person by another and exhorts workers to end it. The burden is on the proletariat to rise up and lose the chains of bourgeois bondage that bind them. Following socialism, the final stage of history under communism will lead to an end to income inequality.

The story of Marx is instructive because it illustrates that moral reflection does not inevitably result in a vision of a social order that works. There are no successful examples of a Marxist utopia, and there are numerous examples of communist efforts that have significantly privileged only a small portion of society. Moreover, in several instances communist collectivization has led to famine and liquidation for millions of people. A Marxist might say that a true Marxist revolution has not yet occurred, but the prospects for such an event seem dim at best. Moral reflection and moral fervor can lead to opposite outcomes. Reflection is dialogical and open to constant review. It must be concerned with process as well as outcomes. To stay relevant, it requires regular input about the changing social environment. For this reason, moral reflection is important to ground economic deliberations at the methodological and policy level. Perhaps, by default, Marx has helped make this clear.

Thorstein Veblen

Marx's vision of concentrated capital seemed on its way to realization in the United States in the final decades of the nineteenth century. The U.S. economy had become heavily dependent on the performance of concentrated industries such as steel, oil, and the railroads. This era, often called the Gilded Age, featured entrepreneurial ventures that amassed huge fortunes and resulted in extravagant lifestyles. The Carnegie, Rockefeller, and Vanderbilt families became symbols of economic success as they spearheaded strong economic growth in leading sectors of the economy. At the same time, labor unions were organizing in the industrial and light-manufacturing sectors, seeking to obtain a greater share of the wealth. A keen observer of the economic and social changes of the Gilded Age was Thorstein Veblen, the economist who in many ways founded

American institutionalism and whose evolutionary economics continues to shape this school of thought.

Veblen's detached personal style of observation and writing and his unconventional lifestyle set him apart in the United States at the turn of the century. Unemployed for seven years after his graduate training, Veblen eventually found his way onto the faculty at the University of Chicago. There he won national recognition as a social critic of the economic behavior of the wealthy. From Chicago, Veblen went on an extended journey as an academic vagabond, teaching at Stanford University, the University of Missouri, and the New School for Social Research in New York City. All the while, he continued to apply his biting satirical skills and critical economic perspective in seeking to explain the conventions that characterized American economic life.

Certainly Veblen's contributions go beyond mere social criticism, for he set out to remake mainstream economic theory. Veblen was influenced by the German historical school with its emphasis on the use of inductive methods in economic investigations. Veblen believed that the deductive reasoning of rational choice analysis made economics largely irrelevant. The neoclassical economics that had become dominant in the latter part of the nineteenth century relied too heavily on abstraction in portraying economic decisions. It ignored the realities of economic power and instinctual decision making. Veblen aimed his critique at the rationality assumption of neoclassical marginalism and its conception of human nature. Veblen thought it ignored the complex propensities and habits of individuals by portraying human nature as passive, substantially inert, and immutable (Veblen 1898, 389). He believed it failed to depict the complex instincts driving the economic actions of consumers, workers, and entrepreneurs. By relying on static equilibrium analysis using mathematical tools, neoclassical economic theory failed to understand men and women as active agents.

Veblen's critique was in keeping with the pragmatic revolt against "the formalism of abstract deductive reasoning in the social sciences" led by his contemporaries William James and John Dewey (Spiegel, 624).

Veblen understood economics as an evolutionary science and aimed his focus on the factors driving change in society. Drawing on anthropological concepts, Veblen focused on the customary modes of consumption and production and the enjoyment of leisure time engaged in by people of different classes, social habits, and patterns of thought. These practices he termed institutions. Evolutionary change in society did not follow some design of creation. Rather, it occurred randomly as individuals adjusted their thought and behavior patterns to changes in technology and other features of the economic circumstances they faced.

Veblen rejected the efforts of his contemporaries who drew on Darwinian conceptions to both explain and affirm the capitalist social order. Social Darwinists had affirmed that human struggle was a natural fact and thus that "competition was the law of life" that produced a harmonious and beneficent order. This perspective helped form the idealized neoclassical conception of the free market, understood as "the institutionalized reflection" of the evolutionary tendency to move toward equilibrium by providing a regulating mechanism that governed price and wage levels to the benefit of both sellers and buyers (Diggins, 12–13).

This "deterministic" understanding of change leading to economic harmony troubled Veblen. His observation of giant business trusts, technical specialists, labor unions, and the spending and leisure habits of the wealthy and working classes in the United States during the Gilded Age convinced him that economics was a process without an enduring socially beneficial equilibrium.

Institutions either channeled the innate human instinct to labor in productive ways or served as expressions of vanity and/or predation. Veblen admired the former direction, associated with technological institutions, but he engaged in biting satire of the latter and its ceremonial institutions. The way social patterns could turn something beneficial into a destructive force interested Veblen in all his work. This "Veblenian dichotomy" is "perhaps the most distinctive tool" relied on by institutional economists to this day (Whalen, 89).

In his first and most famous book, *The Theory of the Leisure Class*, published in 1899, Veblen sought to explain the conventions that guided consumer and worker behavior. These conventions were at odds with neoclassical economics that built on Bentham's notion of a pleasure-optimizing economic person. As we have seen, mainstream economics sought to explain this behavior in terms of rational incremental choices made swiftly and based on net additions of pleasure or pain derived from additional units of a good consumed or a number of hours worked. In a provocative essay, Veblen satirized this pursuit:

> The hedonistic conception of man is that of a lightning calculator of pleasures and pains, who oscillates like a homogeneous globule of desire of happiness under the impulse of stimuli that shift him about the area, but leave him intact. He has neither antecedent nor consequent. He is an isolated, definitive human datum, in stable equilibrium except for the buffets of the impinging forces that displace him in one direction or other.
>
> (Veblen 1898, 389)

Veblen also challenged the neoclassical concept of a static equilibrium that ignored the dynamics of consumer and labor excesses. Consumers wastefully purchased to exhibit status, and laborers worked excessively in order to show off their wealth in conspicuous leisure. Capitalists become predators seeking unfair gains that ultimately sabotaged production. For Veblen the social harmony of the idealized neoclassical world was a fiction.

Veblen declared that the leisure class engaged in conspicuous consumption that satisfied neither physical nor intellectual wants but rather involved displays of wealth that communicated prestige and honor. Expensive clothing and luxury cars communicated status, while an appearance of wealth without expending the labor to acquire it implied an uncommon superiority. Wasteful spending confirmed that image. Moreover, Veblen found that conspicuous labor was essentially a duty: "Abstention from labor is not only a honorific or meritorious act, but it presently comes to be a requisite of decency" (Veblen 1983, 41).

Veblen lauded two human instincts in particular, those of workmanship and curiosity (Lekachman, vii). He valued the expression of workmanship as a creative aesthetic desire to contribute meaningfully to life. Work had a certain dignity and honor that technological institutions embodied. Engineers and technicians exhibited the instinct of workmanship in their efforts to bring forth greater output. Veblen dubbed technological innovations "the machine process." Veblen's moral sympathies lay with the engineers and technicians, those closest to the machine process. Economic change was the product of dynamic technological institutions interacting with the static ceremonial institutions associated with business enterprise.

Veblen was concerned that the creative dynamic of the machine process was being stunted in its growth by the rise of industrial monopoly capitalism. The technicians and engineers had no ownership stake in the modern firm, while those who did, often the "absentee owners," had little interest in productive creativity. The motivations driving business owners were distinctly ceremonial, buttressed by static institutions such as property rights and financial intermediaries, and their goal was aimed at financial gain: "The motive of business is pecuniary gain, the method is essentially purchase and sale. The aim and usual outcome is an accumulation of wealth" (Veblen 2007, 20). Ceremonial institutions impinged on the machine process as business owners allied with the captains of finance to pervert it by limiting output in a form of industrial sabotage. While neoclassical thinking held that profits provided a positive incentive for greater production, Veblen believed that absentee owners engaged in financial manipulation by sacrificing the production of goods. Much of his later writing was aimed at exposing the economic waste and suppression of industrial creativity in what he termed "the price system."

Ironically, as critical as he was of the business system, Veblen did not advocate a stricter form of antitrust policy, nor did he believe the solution would come from social institutions parallel to business enterprise such as charities, religious revivals, or civic education. Rather, he placed his hope in the engineers, thinking that eventually a "soviet of technicians" would form who would, through a general strike, eventually "sweep the timeworn fabric of finance and absentee sabotage into the discard for good and all" (Veblen 1963, 90) and replace the price system with a system that would maximize production and creative efficiency. Veblen expressed a modest optimism that such a change in the economic and social order would be realized.

Veblen's contribution to economic thought is significant in that it enhanced the understanding of economics as a process of institutional change. In addition, his challenge to neoclassical economics paved the way for the more extensive incorporation of moral reflection in economic methodology. This is evident in his extended efforts to explain the reasons underlying why consumers and producers behave as they do. Yet Veblen refused to declare any ultimate purpose in human economic activity. He posited no design in the evolution of economic culture and no final purpose to which the evolutionary change of institutions is headed. Modern heterodox economists in the institutional/evolutionary tradition retain this nonteleological orientation in their analysis of markets and the social order, but they see the embedded values in institutional life as worthy of thoughtful reflection.

Friedrich von Hayek

In twentieth-century Europe, Friedrich von Hayek presented a significant challenge to neoclassical economics. Hayek, the most famous disciple of the Austrian economist Ludwig von Mises (and second cousin of the eminent philosopher Ludwig Wittgenstein), won the 1974 Nobel Prize in Economics for his research on the efficiency of different economic systems and the interdependence of social, economic, and legal phenomena. Hayek shared Veblen's view that modeling alternative equilibrium states was not a helpful way of analyzing an economy. Hayek also qualified the assumptions of perfect information by proposing an alternative understanding of the role of knowledge. In addition, he is recognized for exploring the process of competition and the role of moral values in the evolution of habits and rules in the marketplace.

After serving in the Austrian Army in World War I, Hayek did graduate work in law and economics at the University of Vienna. There he participated in the famed 1920s seminar led by Ludwig von Mises. Focusing his early research on theories of money and capital, Hayek formulated an overinvestment theory of the business cycle. In the realm of macroeconomics, Hayek was Keynes's only significant intellectual opponent in England in the 1930s and 1940s. Contrary to Keynes, Hayek understood the economy to be driven by monetary factors. Hayek contended that the Great Depression originated from overinvestment caused by poor management of the money supply by authorities.

Perhaps Hayek is best known for his longstanding, and at times controversial, stance on the infeasibility of socialism. In this regard, Hayek followed the lead of his mentor Mises, whose 1922 work, *Socialism,* declared the impossibility of economic calculation in socialist economies. Mises's argument centered on the lack of private ownership of resources, which could thereby accurately establish resource prices through a competitive market. When the market socialist Oskar Lange in the 1930s responded that central planners could find prices that would clear markets in a "trial and error" process, Hayek developed a cogent response that stressed the role of knowledge. Socialism was practically infeasible, Hayek demonstrated, due to the wide dispersal of specific information on the opportunity cost of resources. As he put it, "To know which kind of information is required to solve a problem does not imply that it can be solved if the information is dispersed among millions of people" (Hayek 1983c, 58). Market socialism would invariably fail in its attempt to manage the economy by mimicking market prices because socialist planners could never accumulate the mass of data needed for the rational allocation of scarce resources. Only the market price system can provide relevant information in a manner that captures the diverse tastes and preferences and technological capabilities of a modern economy. While Hayek's critique of socialism was derided in the 1930s, toward the end of his life in the early 1990s Hayek witnessed the collapse of centrally planned economies in eastern Europe and in what was then the Soviet Union. In his view, this was the outworking of the "fatal conceit" of socialist planning, in not accounting for the practical knowledge that is conveyed through market prices.

As his research progressed, Hayek extended the analysis of the key role of knowledge and planning in an economy. Hayek argued that individuals plan through "the complex of interrelated decisions about the allocation of our available resources. All economic activity is in this sense planning" (Hayek 1983b, 212). Likewise, Hayek emphasized that what matters is *who* does the planning: "It is a dispute as to whether planning is to be done centrally, by one authority for the whole economic system, or is to be divided among many individuals.... [Competition] means decentralized planning by many separate persons" (Hayek 1983b, 213). Furthermore, in contrasting centralized governmental planning with individual planning by participants in the market, Hayek found that the differences lie not merely in the amount of information available to each type of planner but also in the manner and form in which they obtain the knowledge they need. Markets enable the social coordination of resources because they rely on prices that signal specific bits of information. Individuals possess knowledge not in a "concentrated or integrated form but solely as the dispersed bits" of incomplete information (Hayek 1983b, 212).

Hayek extended his argument regarding knowledge to the question of market equilibrium. Since market participants rely on information specific to their setting, information that is inherently not perfect, market equilibrium is constantly being disturbed as they gain new information (Hayek 1937, 42). This is the "unorganized knowledge of the particular circumstances of time and place" (Leube, xxiii). Such knowledge may be acquired and applied as well by intuition and moral sensibility.

Hayek's perspective on knowledge leads him to spurn the atomistic model of competition and instead see competition as a process of discovery. Given the limits of knowledge possessed by any one individual, Hayek declares that it is the nature of the process of competition to discover "how scarce or valuable" products are (Hayek 1983a, 256). Planning by any individual alone cannot guarantee that resources are allocated to their most valued uses in coordination with the individual plans of others. Only the market as a whole can coordinate all of the varied individual plans of action so that a spontaneous order is achieved. In this way, Hayek offered "an approach that saw the analytical notion of equilibrium fuse with the notion of spontaneous order, and that offered characterization of the economic agent far more complex than the one-dimensional view of Benthamite utilitarianism which led to the notion of *homo economicus*" (Roncaglia, 318). Both Hayek and his mentor, Mises, spurned *homo economicus*, while at the same time placing "human choosers" at the fulcrum of their analysis (Boettke, 161). Hayek finds that a spontaneous order that is socially beneficial arises in an undersigned manner out of human decisions, yet unlike Smith, Hayek is not willing to attribute the source of the underlying design or purpose to God.

Hayek's moral sympathies are oriented to a market economy because he finds that without coercion or planning it generates a beneficial social order. Hayek affirms the superiority of the norm of liberty in his defense of markets and critique of collectivist planning, whether it be expressed in fascism or socialism. A rationalistic faith in scientific advance that Hayek termed scientism seemed to have played a role in encouraging certain twentieth-century governments to rely on central economic planning. In his most famous work, *The Road to Serfdom*, published in 1944, Hayek offers an unflinching moral critique of the tendency of centrally planned economies to be matched with totalitarian political systems. Planners inevitably direct by force virtually every dimension of an individual's life, including where one works, how long one works, and the vocation or profession one is engaged in. A planned society is necessarily coercive because the government planner believes all such decisions must be coordinated with the central economic plan, and the force of the state is invariably needed to ensure such coordination.

Hayek's moral argument for freedom is grounded in the central idea of human ignorance (Hayek 1955, 53). No one planner, whether a government bureaucrat or market participant, can ever obtain all the needed information. Instead market participants must be, as

Klein suggests, *"rule followers,* responding to price signals within a system selected by a process of evolution—a spontaneous order, rather than a system deliberately chosen; yet their actions bring unintended benefits for the system as a whole, benefits that *could not* have been rationally predicted" (Klein, 7). Individuals follow rules, for the most part not knowing the impact of their decisions on others. For Hayek, they must be free to act in this way so that the social norms that have evolved produce the desirable social benefits.

The heterodox economics of Veblen and Hayek share a common emphasis on the importance of understanding the evolution of human customs and habits and their significance for economic decisions (Leathers 1990). Like Veblen, Hayek understands institutional development as an evolutionary process. Human economic behavior follows patterns, rules, and habits so that information does not need to be stored on every activity we engage in. Hayek goes further than Veblen in positing that a social order evolves in ways that are not planned by strictly rational agents.

As people solve problems by a process of intuition and moral sense, social norms develop. The legal structure recognizes this process and helps to keep the social order stable but not fixed, since some norms disappear over time while others persist. Hayek suggests that a kind of "natural selection" process exists in the adoption of a "moral code in the development of the civil order" (Caldwell 2004, 280). Because of the high valuation he places on individual liberty, Hayek endorses a legal structure that gives individuals freedom to discover what they do not know about entrepreneurial possibilities, job opportunities, and products in the marketplace.

Hayek's uplifting of the norm of freedom is tinged with a certain irony. He engages in reflection on the origins of moral norms, but sometimes shies away from explicit moral reflection. It is true that Hayek is willing to appeal to the key virtues upon which an "individualist society rests." He esteems virtues such as "independence, self-reliance, and the willingness to bear risks, the readiness to back one's own conviction against a majority, and the willingness to engage in voluntary co-operation with one's neighbors," affirming that "[c]ollectivism has nothing to put in their place" (1972, 213). For this reason, it is intriguing that, as discussed in chapter 5, the horrendous consequences of collectivist economies led a number of economists in the twentieth century to be disillusioned with the use of economics for activist public policy. They were drawn to logical positivism—arising from the same milieu of 1920s Vienna in which Hayek operated—which separated fact and value in economic analysis. Some economists suggest that Hayek employed the fact-value distinction at times, but at other points he appealed to the norm of liberty, for example, in criticizing socialist theory. The degree to which this alleged inconsistency is true of Hayek and the neo-Austrian school in regard to economic theory remains the subject of scholarly debate.

The spirit of moral reflection remains strong in heterodox economics. Each of the three economists examined in this chapter has established his legacy in a heterodox school of thought that continues in its own particular manner to engage in moral reflection, whether it be radical political economy, evolutionary economics and institutionalism, or neo-Austrian economics. Each of these modern schools offers its own critique of rational choice analysis. The limitations of the rational choice model are examined in the following chapter.

KARL MARX: CAN A MATERIALIST PRODUCE A MORAL CRITIQUE OF CAPITALISM?

In light of a twenty-first-century global financial crisis, Karl Mark's thought is enjoying a bit of recrudescence. Writing as a severe critic of the social consequences of the first Industrial Revolution, Marx understood advanced capitalism to be subject to increasing business instability and failures, surging unemployment, and worsening financial calamities as the business cycle found lower and lower troughs. His predictions concerning inevitable and progressively more severe levels of economic distress resonate with modern critics of global capitalism. They suggest that Marx was correct in emphasizing excessive financial speculation and unrestrained pursuit of profits funded by unsustainable leverage as the source of rapid and widespread economic contractions in economies across several continents.

As economic instability persists and worsens, Marx's analysis of capitalism will likely be more widely explored. He affirms that the dynamics of the capitalist mode of production at its core originate in the drive of the bourgeois capitalist for profit realized by tapping and exploiting economic advantages held over others. Readers of Marx will find that he is an unabashed materialist, contending not only that it is the material mode of production that moves history but also that there is no ultimate reality beyond the material world.

When one delves further into Marx's voluminous writings, it is perhaps surprising to see that he sometimes expresses his critique of the capitalist in strongly moral terms drawn from Christian writers who were inherently nonmaterialist. Marx excoriates the members of the bourgeoisie as rapacious individuals who exploit their workers, the proletariat. Thus in explaining the phenomenon of capital accumulation, he speaks of its source in "exploited human material," finding in the Protestant reformer Martin Luther an affirmation of this tendency of the capitalist, whose "love of power is an element of the desire to get rich" (Marx, *Capital*, 740). Marx sees Luther's critique of the usurer who "eats up, robs, and steals the nourishment of another" as illustrative of the immoral actions of the "capitalist upstart" who ineluctably goes through the historical stage of being driven by "avarice, and the drive for self-enrichment" (Marx, *Capital*, 740–741). Instead of loving his neighbor, the capitalist exploits him through the thievery of an economic system centered on private property and wage labor.

Marx called for the abolishment of private property and the elimination of the capitalist's exclusive control of the means of production. He believed that a proletarian revolution would inexorably accomplish these tasks once capitalism reached a highly advanced stage. Then it would be replaced by a socialist "dictatorship of the proletariat," bringing about the end of economic and financial volatility. Unfortunately Marx wrote in little detail about the institutions that would characterize a socialist economy. This means that he failed to address how the avaricious bent in human nature, reflective of the fact that "original sin is at work everywhere," would somehow be redirected in the "new economic man" toward benevolent ends (Marx, *Capital*, 740).

Perhaps we would expect that Marx the materialist, in the end, would not elaborate on how a moral transformation of human nature could be brought about through changing economic and social arrangements. For it is evident that any moral critique of capitalism must ultimately be grounded in some transcendent moral vision. Ironically, since Marx's materialist worldview could not provide the foundation for his moral critique of capitalism, he needed to borrow the language of Christianity's decidedly moral understanding of human economic activity to articulate his case.

Questions for Discussion

1. Is capitalism by its nature driven by the greed of capitalists?
2. Do you believe Marx's analysis of capitalism is particularly apt in light of recent financial crises in the United States and other market-based economies? Explain.
3. Will market-based economies likely become increasingly subject to boom-and-bust cycles of greater depth and duration? Could a fundamental change in economic institutions enable them to avoid or at least ameliorate such volatile economic swings? Explain.

Chapter 7

On Methods and Morals

Ambiguity is part of the human condition. People have different preferences, values, and perspectives. Everything seems to require judgments, and language possesses so many nuances. Those things that are defined seem to be so by definition. The grass is green because somewhere someone defined what grass looks like as green. The line between subjective and objective is blurred at best and nonexistent at worst. In such a world, how do people make sense of what is going on around them?

William K. Tabb suggests that economists make sense of the world in one of two ways. He claims

> it is useful to arrange economists into A social *science* economists, and B *social* science economists. The A group takes physics as its model. Not modern physics, with its interest in chaos and complexity, but seventeenth-, eighteenth-, and nineteenth-century physics, bolstered by a theorem-driven mathematical fundamentalism. The B science (which ironically is more like modern physics than is A type economic science) is historical, institutional, and comparative.
>
> (Tabb, 18–19)

Mainstream economics throughout the twentieth century was decidedly aligned with the A group. When faced with the complex, interdependent, and changing world, these proponents sought to simplify by finding consistent patterns of behavior derived from primary innate motivations. Individual egoism became the focus of behavioral analysis, and on that foundation a system of resource allocation was built that was defined to be efficient and even fair in many respects. The construction of this system required numerous assumptions and presuppositions that together formed what is called rational choice economics. These assumptions and presuppositions include:

1. Both the natural and social worlds have a consistent design that follows systematic patterns and continuous functions that see behavior as incremental. Nature makes no sudden turns in economics.

2. Those patterns are discernable if the proper techniques of research are followed, and so tentative predictions of future behavior are possible from the models developed.

3. The individual is the key building block of the social order, and people are part of the time-space components studied by physical scientists. A human is referred to as a self-maximizing entity called *homo economicus*. Philosophically, the rational choice process is referred to as economic naturalism.

4. Personal pleasure defined in terms of objectives common to most is the best goal to use when predicting human activity. Values underlying one's utility function are irrelevant to economic analysis.

5. Nuances that qualify utility and make it contextual are largely ignored. A person's utility function is given a priori, is exogenous to the system, and is assumed to be maximized in an individualistic manner.

6. Observable behavior alone is the indicator of one's preferences. Intentions, longings, dreams, or hopes that cannot

be measured in behavior are not helpful in predicting behavior.

7. Variables that are not quantifiable are ignored or assumed constant. The system must be objective and amenable to mathematical deductive and inductive analysis. Any proposition that cannot be tested does not become part of accepted economic theory.

8. Economic actors function within the natural constraints of scarcity and institutional rules of the system that should be based on freedom and natural rights. Principles of resource allocation, distribution, and morality are treated as built-in systemic components rather than viewed as socially formed.

It is important to realize that this rather stark description of the rational choice methodology has limited objectives. Rational choice does not attempt to explain the world, nor does it describe how people actually live. Rather, rational choice provides a model that, in many settings, predicts economic behavior better than alternative models. As such, the methodology is an important tool in the arsenal of those who address economic problems. Its ability to illuminate the possibilities in certain situations must not be minimized, but neither should its shortcomings and limitations be overlooked. The claim in this chapter is that rational choice, as the one dominant tool in the economist's tool kit, has crowded out some other complementary considerations that would enhance the study of human resource provisioning.

One might contrast the task of economic theory building by thinking metaphorically about car manufacturing and maintenance. Is economic analysis like building a car on an assembly line with a clearly defined process that results in a finished automobile

in a predictable time and place, or is economics like auto maintenance in that one must constantly be cleaning, fixing, and replacing
worn-out parts at various times as problems arise? In the manufacturing mode, there is a predictable routine with all the pieces fitting
together in a cumulative fashion until the car is complete. In the
repair mode, there is no end point and there can never possibly be
one. What needs to be done depends on the environment, the social
context, and the goals of those using the car. The manufacturing
mode is a cumulative process through which the finished product
is all that is of interest to the car owner. The maintenance mode
is more of an evolving process and the history of earlier repair is
important to understanding current strategies. Economic analysis
involves frequent maintenance and attention to the social context
and moral climate so that it can address the hidden relationships
that affect the pressing questions of the age. Unfortunately, much
of economic theory building is of the manufacturing variety where
the search for the perfect assembly line of ideas is paramount.

Roger E. Backhouse describes how economics differs from the
other social and human disciplines because of its search for hidden economic principles embedded in the social order. Describing
many contemporary economists, Backhouse states:

> In their view, economics has developed techniques of analy-
> sis that differentiate it sharply from 'soft' disciplines, such as
> philosophy, political science, sociology, history and most of the
> humanities. In such disciplines there are perennial issues over
> which people argue: it is the absence of progress that means
> one can learn, say, political philosophy by studying Hobbes
> and Locke. Economics, in contrast, is believed to have moved
> beyond this stage, the application of mathematical techniques
> having transformed the subject into a cumulative discipline,

in which progress is self evident to anyone familiar with the literature....Unlike philosophers or political scientists, the cumulative nature of the discipline means that economics can be undertaken without knowledge or understanding of the writings of previous generations.

(Backhouse, 3–4)

Backhouse is clearly placing contemporary mainstream economics in the car manufacturing mode. The analytical techniques that Backhouse speaks of involve deductive mathematical model building and inductive verification of hypotheses. These tools, used with a rational choice foundation provide an aura of scientific precision that has captured several generations of economists. Leading journals in the discipline require the reader to have a high level of mathematical proficiency, and nearly all PhD economics programs require the successful completion of several advanced math courses as a condition for acceptance.

Ironically, many economists openly admit that the discipline has lost its moorings and been dominated by mathematical techniques. Peter Bauer has complained that much of the recent economic literature is out of touch with reality because of an infatuation with mathematics. He writes: "The appropriate procedure is, however, to reason to mathematics, rather than from mathematics. But, as highly qualified practitioners have argued, mathematical methods and formulations have run riot in economics without proper appreciation of their limitations" (Bauer, 19).

More than two decades ago, Jack Hirshleifer observed that a better interface between economics and other disciplines was needed. "While scientific work in anthropology and sociology and political science and the like will become increasingly indistinguishable from economics, economists will reciprocally have to become aware of how constraining has been their tunnel vision about the nature of man and social interactions. Ultimately, good economics will also have to be good anthropology and sociology and political science and psychology" (Hirschleifer, 53).

Unless a more holistic approach to economic analysis becomes part of the economist's tool kit, the social and cultural richness that comes from a contextual, historical, and interdisciplinary methodology will continue to be lost and our understanding of how the social order evolves will be lacking. Douglas North makes this point forcefully. "It is essential to remember that the constructs humans create are a blend of 'rational' beliefs and 'non-rational ones' (superstitions, religions, myths, prejudices) that together shape the choices that are made. Our task is to understand the way belief systems evolve and the complicated social structures that have evolved as a consequence; more than that, we attempt an understanding of the way the structure is evolving over time" (North, 83). Predicting without understanding gives little direction going forward as society evolves and attempts to adjust to new realities.

Yet the qualification of rational choice goes substantially beyond its rational one-dimensional approach to human behavior. The fact-value distinction that is embedded in rational choice is problematic in practice. Many variables in economic analysis have subjective content requiring interpretation. For example, unemployment figures involve judgments about search efforts and a definition of how much work constitutes employment. Frequently the most interesting data is constructed in ways that require careful definition and judgments that presume a set of prior conditions based on subjective values. This need not mean that the values in question have significant moral content, but movement from a value-free claim to more subjectively framed data moves the discussion away from the positive/normative dichotomy to more reflective observations and conclusions about the issue being considered. Richard Easterlin provides an example in an article that examines worldwide living standards. Easterlin's research project required him first to choose variables that he felt reflected differences in living standards. The categories of measurement listed come from survey data derived from asking people about their sources of well-being. He then tried to "assemble some rough indicators of various dimensions of the standard of living— arguments, so to speak, of the utility function—without attempting to combine them into an overall measure" (Easterlin, 9). After commenting extensively on the data available to him and recognizing its shortcomings, he is reluctant to use the data as a predictor of the future. "Of course, any serious projections of the future would need to be based, not on mechanical extrapolations of past trends, but on an understanding of the forces driving the advance in living standards and we are far from that nirvana" (Easterlin, 23). While the article is informative and helps one sort through the complexity of the topic, it does not employ mathematics or econometrics as the tool of rhetoric. With simple data charts and a feel for the subjectivity of the data, Easterlin makes a convincing case for progress. The final sentence of the article echoes one concern of this book: "In seeking to understand the wealth of nations, Adam Smith drew deeply on his knowledge of the past. If economics were to return to the study of history, it might conceivably gain better insight into the factors that have shaped this remarkable new world of the 21st century" (Easterlin, 24).

Some research problems lend themselves more to data analysis than others, but few problems have data that is not subjective and open to value judgments. Rational choice economics is far less value free than it would seem when it comes to inductive work. Consequently, its proclamations appear to be far more definitive than is appropriate, and mainstream policy debates focus on critiques of the statistical tools or the completeness of the data rather than on competing social visions. However, there are competing viewpoints increasingly gaining credence that are pressing the main-stream with the claim that economics is not an embedded system to be discovered, that it is historical and contextual in nature, and that it is value laden rather than value free. David L. Prychitko states the problem in its starkest form. "The entire equilibrium-based model is open to serious reexamination and criticism. Indeed, the status of economics as a *science* itself, and its potential as an apriori, value-free theory is in dispute" (Prychitko, 4).

Some will point to welfare economics as an area where the discipline deals with philosophical issues of what is good and how that question applies to interpersonal utility comparisons. By adopting Pareto optimality as a standard, all changes that make someone better off without hurting another will increase social welfare and should be undertaken. Using this logic, utility possibility frontiers and social welfare functions are constructed to show how societal utility can be maximized. Because a social welfare function shows how much utility can be exchanged among people without altering overall social welfare, it is difficult to see how distributional values can be avoided in this analysis. The Pareto optimal social welfare effort is questionable from both a philosophical and rational choice perspective if values are excluded from the analysis. Hilary Putnam summarizes the problem economists have in attempting to couple welfare theory with rational choice methodology:

> Pareto optimality is, however, a terrible weak criterion for evaluating socioeconomic states of affairs. Defeating Nazi Germany in 1945 could not be called Pareto optimal, for example, because at least one agent—Adolf Hitler—was moved to a lower utility surface. Moreover, if the reason for favoring Pareto optimality as a criterion is that one approves of the underlying value judgment that every agent's right to maximize his or her

utility is as important as every other's, then it would seem that Pareto 'optimality' isn't a value neutral criterion of optimality at all.

(Putnam, 56)

Why, one might ask, is such a neatly structured system being questioned now? During its heyday in the twentieth century, economists never claimed it described or explained how the real world actually worked in detail. The claim was that it could predict behavior more accurately than alternative models. As Milton Friedman argued, the neoclassical model is able to predict instrumentally "as if" the economy functioned as stipulated in the assumptions (M. Friedman, 24). In reality, the economy might operate with entirely different dynamics that are as yet unexplained. With such a justification, the most convincing challenge would come from evidence that the predictions made are not accurate. A second challenge could be that, even if the predictions are correct, those being made have lost their relevance because the economic agenda has shifted and the key social questions are now focused on issues where economists have not developed a theory that is helpful. Each of these topics will be treated in turn.

The predicting of rational choice has never been evaluated with the precision required in most economic studies. Commenting on Friedman's instrumentalist methodology, Herbert Gintis makes the following claim: "Indeed, generations of economists learned that the accuracy of its predictions, not the plausibility of its axioms, justifies the neoclassical model of homo economicus. Friedman's general position is doubtless defensible, since all tractable models simplify reality. However, we now know that predictions based on the model of the self-regarding actor often do not hold up under empirical scrutiny, rendering the model inapplicable in many contexts" (Gintis et al. 6–7). Thus, it seems as if the contexts in which *homo economicus* does not apply are growing rapidly as new research considers the impacts of alternative explanations related to findings in the other social sciences and biology. Some of these findings involve rather than exclude moral discernment.

Ironically, there are almost no standards by which to judge the accuracy of rational choice predictions and very little evidence that those predictions would pass the scientific standards of proof required in econometric analysis. There is no study proclaiming that microeconomic equilibrium models are more accurate predictors than common sense approaches to an issue. All we have is the existence of general equilibrium analysis and the belief that anything that exists must be worth its keep or it will shortly disappear. However, that belief itself is founded on assumptions of perfect competition and perfect information made within the neoclassical framework. There is little evidence showing how well mainstream economics predicts or how it compares with other methods of behavioral analysis. Arjo Klamer makes this point by suggesting that "Economists have studied every conceivable human activity but their own. One might logically conclude that those able to become "scientific" about the "rationality" of marriage and suicide might want to become scientific about the rationality of their own doings" (Klamer, 13).

Microeconomist Alan Kirman is more direct in questioning whether mainstream theory predicts well:

If we consider two standard criteria for a scientific theory—prediction and explanation—economic theory has proved to say the least inadequate. On the first count, almost no one contests the poor predictive success of economic theory. The justifications given are many but the conclusions are not even the subject of debate. On the second count, there are many economists who would argue that our understanding of how economies work has improved and is improving and would therefore contest the assertion that economic theory, in this respect, has proved inadequate. The evidence is not reassuring, however. The almost pathological aversion to facing economic theory with empirical data at anything other than the most aggregate level is indicative of the extent to which "explanation" is regarded as being a self-contained rather than testable concept.

(Kirman, 8)

If macro models are built on micro foundations they will contain the same problems previously listed plus the additional difficulties associated with the aggregation of data. If a macro model predicts 2.5 percent real growth in a year and the economy grows only 1.5 percent, is that a helpful prediction or not? Would the social order be different if we had not had any model predicting real growth? Would an astute casual observer of online reports and financial magazines come within 1 percent of actual growth if no economic predicting models were available? Could economists have come closer to the actual growth rate if they had focused on more informal historical and intuitive analysis rather than the formal mathematical models? Of course all of these counterfactual questions can never be answered until the counterfactual situations exist and are compared with the macro model forecasting. The point here is not to argue that a more broad based social-political-economic analysis is preferred to neoclassical mainstream economic analysis. Rather, it is to suggest that the case against that hypothesis has not been effectively made. What follows is a discussion of several important areas where *homo economicus* is being qualified.

One area where microeconomic analysis is ill-equipped to deal with change is when the change is revolutionary rather than gradual.

Marginal analysis has been the mainstay of economics since the turn of the twentieth century, and marginalism has proved an effective approach when smooth-flowing functions gravitate toward equilibrium states. Step functions or sporadically discontinuous functions result in indeterminate outcomes, and thus predictions cannot be made as easily. In a rapidly moving world, the relevance of marginal analysis in microeconomics diminishes. Stephen J. Gould challenges the cultural bias of gradualism as a misreading of history. "The history of life, as I read it, is a series of stable states, punctuated at rare intervals by major events that occur with great rapidity and help to establish the next stable era" (Gould, 226). Commenting on this claim, Manuel Castells suggests that "at the end of the twentieth century, we are living through one of these rare intervals in history. An interval characterized by the transformation of our 'material culture' by the works of a new technological paradigm organized around information technologies" (Castells, 29).

In the macroeconomy, recessions seem to occur at unpredictable intervals when bubbles form and eventually burst with people not being given enough warning to make calculated decisions on margins that would allow for modest adjustments in a psychologically stable environment. The recession of 2007–2009 was a disruption that defied gradualism as people attempted to cope with a relatively sudden 30 to 50 percent drop in many stock portfolios and house prices. Bursts of fear or greed are not the hallmarks of informed, reasoned changes on the margin, yet they are often what drive human choices. Thus marginal analysis supplemented by a variety of motivations involving less gradual change should lead to more accurate predictions and a better understanding of how humans make choices. Moral commitments frequently do not lend themselves to incremental trade-offs.

It is important to recognize that the claim here is not that rational choice methods should be eliminated from the economist's tool kit but rather that the tool kit needs complementary input from all the social sciences and natural sciences so that a larger set of motivational forces can be considered. These motivations are essential qualifiers that integrate context, understanding, and the possibility for moral reflection within economic thinking. When social norms, psychological tendencies, habits, and customs are factored in, behavior often appears less rational and marginal analysis becomes less useful. Fixed-utility functions, income levels, relative prices, and marginal analysis do not adequately assess much of human behavior. Sometimes the concept *expectations* becomes the catchall variable that is used to recognize that there are more drivers of behavior than prices and income. In this way, all the motives influencing behavior and disruptive change can be incorporated into economic theory, but important integrative thinking may be shortchanged in the process.

Another conceptual problem with rational choice theory concerns the dynamics of change in the system. Risk taking is a quality of entrepreneurial activity that causes markets to continually adjust resource flow to their best use. However, risk taking is possible only in an environment of incomplete information and where there is a desire for risk absorption. Risk taking, at its core, does not involve careful calculations on the margin where decisions are incremental and information is perfect. Of course in the real world, information is never complete, but in the conceptualization of the system it is inconsistent to suppose both riskaverse and risk-seeking behavior as the norm if there is no way to determine within the system when each type of behavior applies. Risk-seeking behavior, while an important dynamic for market flexibility and growth, requires an increasing marginal utility for money. Yet a diminishing marginal utility for money assumption is necessary for consumer theory to predict well. Balancing these two responses to monetary gain is something that thoughtful social analysis might consider in its analysis of and approach to the economic system.

Suppose that the case for neoclassical prediction accuracy is upheld for a specific period under consideration. The next concern would be whether neoclassical economists are asking the right questions and tackling the most important issues going forward. Again a great deal of subjectivity is involved in entertaining this topic, but it is no secret that the most fundamental questions in economics change from one era to another. As discussed in chapter 2, in the ancient world the level of production was thought to be limited to the subsistence level in the long run. This belief was sustained by the perpetual struggle for survival that followed civilization into the seventeenth century. With stagnant technology and a fairly constant resource and population base, the economic concerns centered on how society would be organized to see that distribution was fair within some notion of what constituted the good and virtuous life. The fact that the Greek philosophers, Jesus, and the medieval scholastics raised strong questions about the acquisition of wealth made perfect sense in their contexts. The key questions were distribution related, and the answers were found in moral philosophy and social ethics. Because the welfare of the soul and one's eternal destination were of more concern than one's present economic state, the most important question of the times was how material desires could be kept from corrupting the soul.

When production technology slowly began to change and a surplus beyond subsistence became a reality, social analysts started turning their attention to production and its possibilities. Adam Smith used the term *universal opulence* to characterize the kind of social order he envisioned. But such a social order needed a new method of organizing production, a new morality, and a new theory of distribution. The key questions were production based, and technology had to be encouraged. Adam Smith's achievements in the *Theory of Moral*

Sentiments and *The Wealth of Nations* are best seen in light of this need to view social organization in a fresh way so that new concerns could be addressed. However, when production exceeded basic human needs, egalitarian ethics seemed less important and distribution issues were slowly integrated into production theory. Distribution was now dependent more on one's productivity than on some entitlement based on social standing or the need for subsistence. The questions had changed, and economic thinking changed with them. It has evolved from the vision of Smith through the classical economists to the neoclassical theory of today. Along the way, the focus changed from the satisfaction of life's needs to the fulfillment of wants, from steady-state existence to progress and growth.

During the last half of the twentieth century, a new challenge was emerging for economists. The increased speed of technological change brought unprecedented economic growth, but it also created disturbing gaps in the distribution of income within the developed societies and between the developed world and the less developed world. Talk of a new economy began to surface where ideas rather than physical capital drove progress and where increasing returns to production replace the standard diminishing returns constraint. In such a world, the problem of production is thought to be manageable and the economic questions are changed again. While it may never be true that the problem of production is solved, it is possible that it will cease to be the dominant concern in the provisioning of human needs and wants. Distribution and its connection to unemployment, energy availability, and environmental issues may well become center stage or at least join production in importance. Congestion in time and space will make allocation issues more controversial. These issues require increased interaction with the moral and ethical disciplines and other social sciences. For example, if parents can pick the gene combinations of their children at a very low cost, how will the preferred combinations be allocated or can everyone be granted

ON METHODS AND MORALS

their optimal choice? Of course the choice could be left to the free market where the demand for the preferred genes would increase the gene price lowering its net return. Such a system would require considerable change in how people think about income distribution.

If technology advances as projected and competes with the human mind as an efficient producer, then output will be less a function of human input and the marginal productivity theory of distribution will need to be reworked or discarded. The impact of technological advance on economic theory could be enormous as it alters the key questions that economists entertain. Because of these trends, a narrowly focused rational choice methodology may be inadequate to deal with the coming realities. It is important now to recognize that a considerable amount of recent work has been done to broaden the scope of economics and make it more relevant to the world as people observe it. Outcomes that do not conform to rational choice analysis are becoming increasingly apparent and interesting.

So far the analysis of rational choice has focused on issues raised in past decades. These methodological discussions have continued since the logical positivism debates of the early twentieth century. The resistance to interdisciplinary research is rapidly breaking down. By engaging in experimental practices and exploring neurobiology, psychology, sociology, the efficiency of law, cooperation, and the nature of trust in behavior, economists have opened the door to moral issues that were not thought to be relevant in positive analysis. The next chapter looks at ways this broader approach to economics has brought moral questions to the center of economic work.

JOHN MAYNARD KEYNES

It seems that every time the economy goes into a recession people look for bailouts, stimulus packages, tax cuts, and new government spending programs on infrastructure or other public works projects. On the other hand, when times are good, government intervention is often considered harmful for market capitalism because the markets will adjust successfully without intervention. If monetary authorities keep the money supply growing at a rate near the growth of real output, prices should be stable and full employment should be maintained. Why do markets seem to work better on the upside of the business cycle than on its downside?

More than any other economist, John Maynard Keynes explored these questions and, against the backdrop of the Great Depression of the 1930s, came up with answers that have been used in all subsequent recessions including the most recent one in 2008 and 2009. The stimulus packages of both Presidents George W. Bush and Barack Obama fit Keynes's policy suggestions well. So what did Keynes discover that was new?

First, Keynes put more emphasis on psychology than earlier economists did. People save money when they fear hard times are coming. Even very low interest rates will not encourage much spending or discourage saving if consumers feel insecure about their jobs. In Keynes's words, "Because, partly on reasonable and partly on instinctive grounds, our desire to hold Money as a store of wealth is a barometer of the degree of our distrust of our own calculations and conventions concerning the future" (Keynes 1937, 216). Consequently, individuals resist or reduce their spending when fear takes over.

Firms will also not expand their businesses no matter how cheap loans become if they are concerned about their future profits because they already have excess capacity due to reduced consumer spending. Speaking about the tendency of firms to pull back from spending, Keynes states that "[W]hen a more pessimistic view is taken about future yields, that is no reason why there should be a diminished propensity to hoard" (Keynes 1937, 218). The psychology of fear and pessimism drive spending and investment. In a recessionary environment, monetary policy aimed at lowering interest rates is likely to fail because individuals and firms do not spend available money. This claim was a devastating blow to those who argued that changing relative prices could keep an economy on track. Keynes was convinced that, left on its own, markets in a capitalist economy can spiral downward rather than self-correct in times of recession.

In a second, related claim, Keynes argued that putting money in people's pockets rather than lowering interest rates would increase spending. In his words, "People's propensity to spend (as I call it) is influenced by many factors such as the distribution of income, their normal attitude to the future, and—though probably in a minor degree—by the rate of interest. But in the main the prevailing psychological law seems to be that when aggregate income increases, consumption-expenditure will also increase but to a somewhat lesser extent" (Keynes 1937, 219). He claimed that people spend a fairly constant proportion of their income so a tax cut or lump-sum grant would stimulate the economy as spending rises. Thus the role of public spending can help to offset reduced private spending in recessions, though the exact amount of the resulting stimulus to aggregate expenditure remains a controversial topic among macroeconomists.

Keynes summed up his policy recommendation by saying: "I conceive, therefore, that a somewhat comprehensive socialization of investment will prove the only means of securing an approximation to full employment; though this need not exclude all manner of compromises and of devices by which public authority will co-operate with private initiative" (Keynes 1965, 378). It is not surprising that those committed to laissez-faire capitalism opposed Keynes for decades and still consider Keynesian economics to be socialism in disguise, even though he made it clear that he did not approve of pubic ownership of production capital. He felt public stimulus would encourage private owners of capital to invest again.

Whatever one's political and economic views are, it is clear that from Keynes's time onward public expenditure to stimulate a slow or recessionary economy has become a regular practice in market economies. In recent years George W. Bush and Barack Obama put into place stimulus policies that relied on government spending hoping to move a stagnant economy toward full employment. Both were following the legacy in economic theory and practice left by John Maynard Keynes.

Questions for Discussion

1. How much of your economic behavior is influenced by fear and pessimism when recessions occur?
2. Explain why lower interest rates do not seem to stimulate an economy as much as money put in the hands of consumers.
3. Do you fear that recessionary stimulus packages are making our economy more debt ridden and socialistic?

Chapter 8

Expanding and Reorienting the Scope of Economic Thinking

In the last chapter, the rational choice method of approaching economic decisions was discussed with some attention to its tendency to limit moral reflection. This chapter begins with some examples of how rational choice has been extended and now is being altered as new frontiers in social thinking emerge. Shoshana Grossbard-Shechtman and Christiopher Clague describe some of these efforts to enrich the discipline as expanding and reorienting economics (Grossman et al., 7–11). The expansion of economics, as described by Grossbard-Shechtman and Clague, involves applying rational choice thinking beyond the traditional domain of economic analysis. On one level, this seems to extend rational choice methodology as the reigning tool of economic behavior analysis. However, it also opens the door to a wider range of behavior, much of which needs a more complex analysis than single motivation thinking. Ronald Coase and Oliver Williamson recognized that information is not free to firms and that the exchange process involves time, energy, and a host of other possible impediments that can lead to inefficient outcomes. For them, the firm is more than a site of mechanical interactions with zero transaction costs. Economists such as James Buchanan, Douglas North, and Gordon Tullock began to analyze political institutions, arguing that political behavior can be predicted by assuming that politicians operate more out of their own interest than out of some view of public service.

Richard Posner and Ronald Coase have shown how the law can be evaluated by its contribution to efficiency as defined in economic terms. Gary Becker and others have looked at marriage and family life in terms of mutually beneficial exchange contracts, and Laurence Iannaccone and others have explored religious behavior using a rational choice approach. In nearly all these cases, there is the presumption that institutions are a composite of individuals who act rationally to form groups designed to solve a joint production problem of some kind. Marriages last as long as the net benefits exceed the net benefits of an alternative arrangement. People participate in churches as consumers, not producers, and politicians promote the public good only when it is in their personal interest to do so. New institutionalism is the label often given to these projects designed to broaden economics by extending rational choice analysis beyond individual material provisioning into other institutions of the social order. Little attention is given to the notion that the institutions of marriage, church, and politics have social power to form individuals and influence behavior. William Tabb describes the contrast well: "In general, the new institutionalists focus on the ways individuals create institutions and emphasize formal techniques, whilst the old institutionalists describe how institutions mold individuals and employ non-formal techniques" (Tabb, 123).

It is important to ask how these efforts to extend economics have influenced the discipline's prospects for moral reflection in its analysis. In this regard, there appears to be good news and bad news. On the positive side, economics is venturing into areas where values traditionally have been important, and so the values-based questions keep seeping into the discussion. When marriage is conceptualized as a comparative advantage and exchange arrangement, it is difficult to explain why at least half of marriages last, because most successful marriages will attribute their endurance to commitment, willingness to sacrifice, and a belief that it is not right to seek more desirable alternatives when the going gets tough. Rational choice analysis of religious activities forces the researcher to make judgments about what is the appropriate data and what is the meaning of the outcomes. Statesman and patriots who give up personal comfort for public benefit cause new institutionalists to ponder the dynamics of such action. Thoughtful reflection is inevitable in this venture, unless one is satisfied with meaningless correlations of unexplored data. These examples illustrate that new institutionalism has prompted economists to venture into areas more affected by moral content than traditional economic analysis of the consumer and the firm entailed. Prediction alone is hardly enough. Perhaps the limits of rational choice analysis will become more apparent as conversation with other disciplines occurs. The negative side of the new institutionalist expansion of economics is that, by downplaying the social and moral components of institutional life, rational choice analysis misses the rich dynamics of how a social order is formed and how the institutions of a society provide stability, meaning, and purpose that go beyond autonomous individualism.

While the expansion of economics has heightened awareness of moral reflection, it is the reorienting (as described by Grossbard-Shechtman and Clague) more than the expansion of economics that has given moral reflection a place at the economist's table. It is no accident that economics was born during the time when the search for scientific truth extended to all areas of life. As the scientific worldview gained acceptance, social science became fragmented into its constituent parts so that more careful analysis could be performed without the clutter of unmanageable variables. Economics led the way, perhaps because of its quantifiable nature, toward a value-free positivistic approach to learning. Earlier chapters have illustrated how, after

1860, mainstream economics began moving from the wide-ranging long-run metanarrative approach of Adam Smith to a mathematical analysis of individual utility in search of a short-run prediction of relative prices and their influence on consumer behavior. For purposes of analysis, people functioned as maximizers of individual utility, driven primarily by changes in relative prices and personal income. By 1920, the discipline had become a microeconomic exercise in price theory with a limited macroeconomic consideration showing the nominal effects of alternate levels of the money supply.

It would be wrong to see this trend in the discipline as being somehow irrelevant or morally questionable. Two factors, in addition to the scientific climate, contributed to these changes. First, as described in chapter 3, the concerns of Adam Smith were largely production related. However, with technological advances and increased production, the key concern of economists turned more toward optimal allocation with given prices and income levels. Because prices were the key regulator of resource flow, it was important to analyze exactly how prices were determined and how they regulated the flows. The long-run price theory of the classical economists was not as helpful as the supply-and-demand analysis of the neoclassical theorists. Deductive mathematical modeling combined with rational choice assumptions provided good tools to assess those flows and the prices that regulated them. Thus, as is usually the case, the pertinent questions of the time led to theories that provide the most straightforward answers to those questions. The more mechanistic approach to economic thinking also reinforced the notion that economics had become a true science. What governed the flow of resources to their best use was the key question, and rational market behavior provided a straightforward and usually helpful answer.

The second reason for the dominance of the neoclassical method is more problematic but related to the first. In an effort to ensure that values and beliefs did not infect the progress of science, a movement toward a positivistic philosophy of science took shape in the 1920s and beyond. This movement, discussed in chapter 5, made economics a respectable science by abstracting significantly from reality and making predictability the primary objective of economic analysis. While deductive theorists concentrated more and more on the nuances of general equilibrium theory and whether general equilibrium was achievable, induction-oriented economists were much more willing to test empirically hypotheses related to policy proposals and to move forward when the probabilities for success were sufficiently high. Establishing scientific economic truth was not the primary objective for empirical analysis, and so an uneasy relationship developed between the inductive and deductive sides of positive economic analysis. A truce of sorts has been established because of the complementary relationship between theory and practice. However, there has been increasing concern that economics may not be as relevant to complicated social problems as it should be because neither camp was willing to venture very far into the subjective nature of economic life. Interdisciplinary work with less scientific social sciences was not highly valued in mainstream circles. Philosophical and moral reflection was even more removed from analysis because its claims were hard to falsify in principle.

Statistical relationships and abstract equilibrium models aimed primarily at prediction often do little to portray the nature of the economy and how it really works. In addition, the speed of change in technology and social organization make correlations of the past seem less relevant to the future. The questions most pertinent also seem to be changing again. The three questions often listed as foundational to economics are: What shall be produced? How shall it be produced? And for whom shall it be produced? Along the way, this book has emphasized how changing times lead to changing questions in economics. If institutional patterns lead to economic growth, the prospects for enhanced production are brought to the forefront. As average incomes rise and technology-driven growth is expected, distribution becomes more important in order to determine who gets the gains generated by the system. If environmental or nonrenewable energy concerns dominate, the focus shifts to how externalities might be internalized. Compared with production efficiency, distribution and environmental questions have more obvious moral overtones. Fairness, social solidarity, and justice seep into the discussion because intergenerational impacts, social costs, and public goods become more prominent in the allocation process. Values, emotions, and social norms begin to crowd into the scientific deliberations, and moral reflection becomes increasingly pertinent. Somehow a much broader long-run approach with interdisciplinary insights is needed to be relevant in rapidly changing times. Wilfred Beckerman makes this point in describing the moral content of decisions made about the intergenerational impacts of economic activity. Beckerman, in a detailed account of how the technical areas of welfare economics can be a bridge between mainstream economics and moral reflection, lists three value-laden issues that must be considered in such work: What constitutes welfare, how is the social discount rate determined, and how valid is it to determine an optimal intergenerational path from the perspective of the first-generation actors? (Beckerman, 9–11). Intergenerational concerns require some thought about the meaning of good beyond the individual preferences of present actors. The area of welfare economics is one where economists have considered philosophical concerns without engaging in the moral discourse that illuminates the topic.

Austrian economists, especially Friedrich Hayek, and American institutionalists, particularly Thorstein Veblen, have qualified the mechanistic approach to economics by considering institutional change and a variety of motivations for economic behavior. The institutionalists opened the door slightly to moral questions in economic methodology, but for the Austrians and those who see markets as spontaneously evolving, the moral issues are not included as a dialogical process. Rather, they are part of a decentralized interaction and, as such, become embedded without intentional design into the market structure. Moral reflection is often relegated to the normative component of economic thinking and viewed as outside the scope of economic theory.

Harold Demsetz's *From Economic Man to Economic System* stands out as an example of this spontaneous view of markets:

> The spontaneous order puzzle asks how a sensible allocation of resources emerges from a setting in which conscious coordination and central planning are absent. All these words suggest a beneficial outcome for the individual and a lack of concern for the larger society, but all the economic model really assumes is that people know and act on what they *want*. What they want is not necessarily good for them or for others. The "sensible" allocation of resources is not to be interpreted to mean socially, personally, or morally correct or incorrect.
>
> (Demsetz, 19)

It is true that, when I shop at a grocery store I do not see my transaction as some moral commentary on the economic system. However, in searching for a meaningful concept of efficiency, it is unfortunate if resources end up in places that make people socially, personally, or morally worse off. The easy answer is to say that all these things are assumed as operative in personal utility functions and are not subject to social dialogue. Accordingly, in modern times the process of utility function formation is located outside the bounds of economics proper.

In addition, because spontaneous market forces create the prices to which the consumer responds, moral dialogue about the content of prices is counterproductive. To engage in moral reflection is to risk coercive outcomes and endless controversy. Yet people do not live their lives in a moral vacuum; so it is important to see how moral reflection might enter the arena of economic analysis. First, exploring the formation of utility functions will become increasingly part of the economist's tool kit as genetic predispositions, psychological propensities, and neuroeconomics teach us more about how we function. Values and beliefs would be a logical additional step toward understanding what is going on in the creation of utility functions. Second, even if utility function formation is ignored, moral concerns lead to shifts in supply-and-demand functions and can enter the discussion as relevant components of market prices and efficiency considerations just as other considerations are analyzed. Isolating moral reflection from economic analysis minimizes the relevance of economics and can lead to inaccurate predictions.

The rigid adherence to the value-free assertion of positive economics and the sterile rational choice mechanism is being tested on many fronts as will be discussed later in the chapter. Even on its own terms, economics has a difficult time claiming that it can be value free. First, it can be readily noted that the notion of individual freedom with independent, unchanging preference patterns involves a value judgment as to what is good and how one should live. Perhaps the most straightforward example of this can be seen in the work of Ayn Rand. In novels and various philosophical writings, Rand develops the concept that the moral life is a purely rational process based on the principle that people are created to seek their own self-interest for the sake of survival. The moral person is neither a predator nor an altruist but pursues production creatively for personal benefit. The result is a social order that can thrive if the values that are formed truly reflect what is beneficial to the individual. Objective calculation will lead to practices that best promote survival, and it is this rational process that leads to the moral life.

Motivations like religion or materialism are not based on rational scientific evidence, and they therefore cannot be relied on as guides to moral behavior nor can they provide sufficient social cohesion on which a viable society can be constructed. In this view, humans contain the necessary rational resources within themselves to live a moral life that will then naturally contribute to their personal survival and a viable social order. There need be no social vision and no common processing of what is good because what one should do for survival is what is morally good. Thus, the issues of what is the meaning of good and what is good behavior merge into one concern: What best promotes my survival as a person?

Rand's objectivism contrasts with a telos-based moral framework that seeks to discern the intentions of a deity or creator outside the individual, but her philosophy involves moral reflection of a purely rational, if not dialogical, nature. If freedom and property rights are protected, the individual pursuit of survival spontaneously creates a system of economic coordination that is desirable. What is lacking is a full accounting of how human interdependence might be sorted out if various individual's survival values and strategies are not fully complementary. For this reason, many look beyond this highly individualized approach to the moral life to a more social conception of what is moral.

Mainstream economists venture into moral issues in welfare economics where the goals of economic activity are entertained. What does economics try to optimize? The standard answer is *utility*, and upon further probing the word, happiness is frequently offered. How happiness is conceived, however, continues to perplex economists. Pierluigi Barrotta has shown how difficult the concept of happiness is to implement both theoretically and practically. Barrotta uses Sigmund Freud as an example. Freud, in failing health and in pain, refused help from drugs because of the way he thought they would dull his thinking capacity. The question for economists is: How can we assess Freud's level of happiness? If we ask him on a questionnaire, he would claim to be happier without the drugs. If we performed a neurological brain scan measuring happiness, he would be shown to be worse off without the drugs because the brain waves would show distress rather than happiness. Yet economists, following a hedonistic approach, value first-person judgments and are inclined to go with the individual survey result:

> For hedonism, in order to establish whether a person is happy or not we have merely to find out a way to detect his or her state of mind. Consequently, hedonists focus on the following question: 'How do people feel?' Freud's case shows us that this way of looking at happiness is at the very least incomplete. We have to add a further characteristic: the set of values through which individuals assess their feelings. These values act as standards: happy people are not only those who feel good, but also those whose life meet some requirements. For pluralism, in order to establish whether people are happy or not we have to focus on the following different question: "Do their lives fulfill the standards freely chosen by them?"
>
> (Barrotta, 154)

This can lead to counterintuitive results. Amartya Sen refers to cases in which people near poverty consider themselves happier than many in richer countries do, meaning that context and relative standing are more important than any given level of comfort. He argues for a broader standard of well-being than first-person happiness measurement. Well-being, as the variable to be maximized, is more complex than a simple self-assessment from a given vantage point, although economists wish to maintain the notion that people are autonomous and can make valid independent assessments of their welfare.

Bruno Frey explores the complexity of happiness as the goal of economic activity. Summarizing his findings, he claims, "Happiness research suggests that individual evaluations are much broader than those enshrined in economic theory. Most importantly, it shows that individuals derive utility not only from income (as is implied in much of received theory) but also from highly valued social relations and from self-determination, as well as using their own competence. Moreover, individuals derive utility from processes, not just from outcomes" (Frey, x).

At the very least, it seems reasonable to recognize that there will be many different sets of value judgments used by people assessing their individual level of happiness. The concepts of a grand utility frontier and a social welfare function, which have always been ambiguous in practice, will need to be qualified recognizing that values and moral reflection cannot be ignored. Economists have always noted that welfare economics brings them as close to philosophy and value judgments as they would like to go. Beckerman makes this point after listing numerous other cases where assumptions of cost-benefit analysis hinder its precision: "But because some of the value judgments implicit in welfare economics are usually only in the background, the extent to which they qualify the whole structure of standard welfare economics is not always adequately appreciated" (Beckerman, 77).

Not only are utility functions ambiguous, but also the notion that each person has an independent utility function is hard to accept. During the last century in the developed Western world, real incomes have risen to the point at which people are freed to pursue objectives further down Maslow's hierarchy of needs. When basic needs are met, concerns about security and self-actualization become important, and many of these needs require a joint production process and cooperative action. Environmental cleanup and income distribution concerns are each examples where this contention is true. In the mid-twentieth century, Harvey Leibenstein pointed out that people have interdependent preference patterns that lead to snob appeal, bandwagon effects, and all kinds of positional externalities (Leibenstein, 111–127). Snob appeal is present when you spurn a better price at a warehouse-type retailer and buy the identical article of clothing at an upscale department store because of what your peers may think of buying clothes at a warehouse store. Bandwagon effects occur when your children will only wear name brand shoes because everyone else at school has them even if generic brands are much cheaper and just as good. An example of positional externalities is when people get into a consumption race to keep from falling behind in social standing.

As we saw in chapter 6, decades earlier Veblen spoke of conspicuous consumption as a driving force in consumer choice making. All of these examples point to interdependent preferences, a characteristic that makes analysis of preference formation an important part of economic research. Such work inevitably leads to moral reflection if preferences are socially formed and nurtured. Again the effect of institutional settings and cultural norms comes into play. Kenneth J. Koford and Jeffrey B. Miller show how social norms, such as reciprocity, or habits, such as when to go to lunch, may simplify decision making in life, but standard rational choice models would not accurately predict them. "Explicit recognition of habit and custom leads to a different behavioral model than economists are accustomed to analyzing, for many actions are not rational (i.e., are not the outcome of some utility calculus); rather they depend on previously constructed patterns of behavior" (Koford and Miller, 23). Jon Elster has explored the development of social norms in depth, and he distinguishes among social norms, moral norms, and quasi-moral norms (Elster, 104). Social norms are behavioral patterns that develop because one's behavior is transparent to others. Quasi-moral norms develop when one can observe other people's behavior

and respond accordingly. Both of these involve interdependent utility functions that can lead to behavior not predicted by rational
choice analysis. Moral norms are unconditional, operating out of a
value system that may put the interests of others ahead of personal
desires. Some religious commitments involve moral norms of this
nature. Elster pursues many nuances of social behavior, illustrating
how much of what we do is conditioned by forces, including beliefs
and moral commitments, that go far beyond what rational choice
methodology considers.

While institutional analysis, Austrian economics, explorations
into happiness and an examination of socially conditioned behavior
have encouraged a reorienting of economics, perhaps the greatest
challenge to mainstream value free methodology comes from efforts
to uncover the way the mind is constructed and how it functions.

Psychology and neuroeconomics are entering economic conversation, and they make moral dialogue unavoidable. Douglas North
makes this point by suggesting that "The most important contribution of the evolutionary psychologist is explicating the underlying inference structure of the mind that appears to account for the
predisposition of the mind to entertain and construct 'nonrational'
beliefs such as supernatural explanations and religions that under-
lie so much of the decision framework of individuals, groups, and
organizations in societies" (North, 30). Daniel Kahneman, Amos
Tversky, Robert Frank, and others have pointed out a host of psychological limitations and emotions that influence behavior in ways
counter to rational choice predictions (Frank 1988; Tversky and
Kahneman 1981). Kahneman, a psychologist, won the 2002 Nobel
Prize in Economics for his work showing that there are significant
areas of behavior that violate rational choice axioms. In his work,
he notes that human behavior rarely is totally open-ended, even if
people are rational choice maximizers. For most, certain limitations exist before any issue is considered. A religious person may

rule out many behavioral options on moral grounds but optimize the remaining possibilities. Psychological constraints often bound rationality as well. Tversky and Kahneman illustrate that people have psychological predispositions that affect behavior. They compartmentalize life in ways that foreclose some options. For example, a movie ticket lost would be considered part of the limited entertainment budget, while the same amount lost in cash on the way to the theater would be considered as a small portion of the total budget. Thus people are not likely to buy another ticket if the ticket was lost, but they are more likely to buy a ticket if it was the cash that was lost. Tversky and Kahneman also found that people weigh losses differently than gains of equal value, so that one would feel worse off at the end of the day if he or she got an unexpected $10 bonus and lost a $10 bill on the way home from work.

In the early 1980s, behavioral economics was viewed as a challenge to mainstream rational choice thinking, but since 1990 there has been an effort to see psychology as a complementary component of economic thinking (Sent 2004). By 1998, a survey article in the *Journal of Economic Literature* documented this movement as one that was being integrated successfully into the mainstream of economic research (Rabin 1998). By opening the door to more complex thinking about human behavior, it becomes possible to consider how moral and ethical commitments are part of the mental processing affecting choices made in markets and elsewhere.

There are other issues that qualify the power of rational choice as economists practice it. In many circumstances, everyone in a group is better off if each member cooperates rather than follows a narrow self-interested course of action. However, if everyone in the group is cooperating, it is in the interest of any single person to cheat on the cooperative agreement. If a small country that is a member of the Organization of Petroleum Exporting Countries (OPEC) continues to keep production high while the other member nations agree to cut production to raise world oil prices, then that small country has an extra benefit of high output and high prices. If everyone keeps production high, the price plunges, making everyone worse off. To solve these problems, there must be a way to establish cooperation, commitment, solidarity, and trust. As Zey observes, "But according to rational choice theory, which assumes self-interested maximizers, there are no values within the individual or forces external to the individual sufficient to make actors keep their commitment or trust. Trust is impossible to establish without some set of values" (Zey, 97).

A substantial literature is developing that recognizes the many areas of life where teamwork or group cooperation results in preferred outcomes. In these areas, moral reflection becomes an ingredient in making joint production work. Consider a neighborhood potluck picnic to which each household brings a dish to share, making the experience a real feast. If, as the masses assemble, there is no way to know who brought food and who did not, *homo economicus* would be materially ahead if he simply attended without contributing. However, if he assumed everyone else would do the same, he might bring a dish to prevent the event from becoming a debacle, which would be a worst-case outcome. However, knowing that his neighbors fear the same outcome and are likely to bring food, he proceeds to attend without food expecting to be the only free rider there. Is the party a success? Most, if not all, such gatherings turn out to be a success, the reason being that *homo economicus's* logic is not followed by most. People feel morally obligated to do their share, and, unlike the public goods case previously discussed, that obligation arises from the personal nature of the interaction. The moral sense that shirking your duty or obligation is wrong makes the system work. Yet there is more to making these situations work than simply sitting in the kitchen and speculating.

A rich literature on cooperative behavior exists. Complex game theory models explore the ramifications of these situations of interdependency attempting to uncover what forces in society help individuals commit to one another and engage in the optimal cooperative behavior without the downside of undesirable coercion. Hervé Moulin explores how microeconomics has considered these cooperation opportunities: "I submit that cooperation between selfish economic agents can be conceived in three fundamental 'modes.' Namely, direct agreement, justice, and decentralized behavior" (Moulin, 3). Direct agreements rely on noncoercive behavior involving negotiation and agreement that then leads to optimal results. Deal making is rational behavior for all parties. Clearly it relates best to smaller groups like neighborhood picnics where negotiation possibilities lead to agreements and institutions in civil society that enhance individual and group welfare. Cooperatives, parent-teacher associations (PTAs), and rules of games like baseball and golf all work because people agree to follow the bylaws, rules, and membership obligations of the group knowing that without cooperation the benefits derived from the group activity will be lost. By careful participant selection and voluntarily chosen enforcement methods, cooperative behavior becomes the norm. Membership lists, umpires, and by-laws become institutionalized leading to the benefits of joint cooperative behavior. Advance sign-up sheets for bringing specific items to the potluck would be a form of direct agreement. For Moulin, direct agreement cooperation is simply wise actions leading to optimal outcomes assuming all the transactions costs of institutional development and monitoring are inconsequential. While such cooperative behavior can be viewed as simply wise action given the alternatives, it is still true that the *homo economicus* out for a free ride would likely stress the system if he or she feels no moral obligation to live up to the agreement. Therefore, purely rational direct agreements may solve some joint production problems, but it is often moral considerations that make the agreements stick.

What Moulin's calls the justice mode of cooperative behavior requires deliberate moral reasoning to be effective. This method posits an arbiter who makes decisions in cooperative settings. According to Moulin, "The arbitrator's decision will leave none of the concerned agents unhappy only if it is perceived as fair. Moreover, they will accept her decision only if they understand the decision-making process" (Moulin, 19). Here the host of the picnic assigns a food category to each neighbor and knows who brings what when the time arrives. If the assignments are viewed as fair, the neighbors willingly participate, knowing that all are doing their share. Perceptions of fairness are complicated because they generally center on simple equality, proportional equality, or stable egalitarianism. Suppose everyone feels fairly treated and the party is a success. Then when dessert time comes a small cake is to be divided between Sean and Ted. It is Ted's favorite kind of cake, but Sean is not particularly fond of it. What is the fair division of the cake between Ted and Sean? Maximizing overall pleasure from the cake would give Ted the bigger piece. The notion of proportional pleasure would dictate that Sean receive the bigger piece, since he needs more to make him as satisfied as Ted will be with a small piece. Apart from a reference to established social norms, more information on the context, and a moral sense, there is no answer to the cake division dilemma. The host's division of the cake must conform to the definition of fairness shared by those involved, and that definition requires considerable moral reflection. For similar reasons, there are no simple answers to how the tasks are shared in any joint production ventures. Consequently, the arbiters in the form of party hosts, elected officials, or corporate managers are successful when their decisions are viewed as just, and to be just they must pass the moral screens of what is considered right and good by all involved. Thus cooperation by rules of justice requires moral reflection in order to arrive at some rule that best serves those involved in the cooperative venture. When governors attempt to balance state budgets by limiting the collective bargaining actions of state employees and that action is viewed as unjust, demonstrations and protests fragment social solidarity. The language from all sides is cast in moral terms of right and wrong, fairness, and the nature of rights rather than in term of social welfare optimization.

Moulin's third category of cooperation examines decentralized behavior as a means to cooperative outcomes. Perfect competition market theory is a good example of social coordination in a decentralized setting where prices determine outcomes. The social good is maximized when participants pursue their best interests. Negotiation costs are limited to finding prices and the small neighborhood party is now a massive urban food festival with vendors selling items for a price. Cooperation exists in that participants follow the rules of the system, and the presumption is that those rules will overcome the coordination problems of the direct agreement and justice types of coordination. However, this abstraction frequently does not fit the world of market concentration, inflexible labor markets, externalities in both production and consumption, and the category of output called public goods.

Elaborate game theory models show how interdependent firms deal with output and pricing decisions, and management-labor relations will frequently evolve around justice and direct agreement forms of cooperation. The same forms are present as society attempts to sort out environmental and other externality concerns.

Economists have always recognized that benefits from some goods and services, once produced, could not be excluded from others who can consume them free of charge. Furthermore, in many of these cases, adding one more consumer did not cost anything additional. Services such as national defense and mosquito control reflect this model and therefore fit under the category of a public good, provided by coerced cooperation through the tax and expenditure system of government. Again, Moulin's direct agreement and justice method of solving social problems come into play.

Thus, moral reflection is intertwined in all of the three scenarios presented by Moulin. Considerations of justice cannot be underestimated because they represent any situation in which people interact, following rules not of their own making. Given the protest against dictators internationally and the demonstrations by workers, retirees and those seeking health care in the United States, considerations of justice seem to be a growing part of resource allocation processes. There is no guarantee that there will be any contemplation of what, in the Aristotelian sense, is really good for the parties involved, but the moral issues will surface in ways that cannot be ignored.

Some may still assert that the case for moral virtues in determining behavior is little more than enlightened self-interest. Early thinkers who theorized about capitalism made those claims frequently, as Hirschman observes, "All the heroic virtues were shown to be forms of mere self-preservation by Hobbes, of self-love by La Rochefoucauld, of vanity and of frantic escape from real self-knowledge by Pascal" (Hirschman, 11). It is hard for economists to see human behavior at the deepest level of motivation as something other than self-aggrandizement because the competitive environment is designed to weed out those who follow other motivations. Cooperators will lose out to those who follow their narrow self-interest in a competitive world.

However, Robert Frank develops a model of cooperative behavior that posits a genuine preference for cooperation, and he shows that there is a place in the world for those who follow that motivation. Using hawks and doves as metaphors for aggressive self-interested behavior and genuinely cooperative behavior, respectively, Frank develops a payoff matrix that generates the highest benefits when two doves work together in a cooperative manner. If two hawks work together, they aggressively dissipate the benefits through competitive behavior. If a hawk and a dove work together, the dove gets little or no benefit because the dove is true to its nature and does not fight for its share. Using the biological assumption that greater benefits lead to faster reproduction, Frank shows that when doves can identify one another easily, it is inevitable that the social order will include both hawks and doves permanently. If doves can easily discern each other the hawks will become extinct because no dove will work with a hawk, leaving hawks fighting among themselves to their own detriment. Given that some cost of discernment is likely, a final equilibrium will result in a mixture of doves and hawks. This, of course, relates only to the portions of the social system that involve joint production with opportunities for cooperation.

What is interesting about the Frank model is that the dove cooperators are behaving out of a different nature from the hawks. They find one another for their own survival, but they inherently seek the overall welfare of the community in their actions. From the point of view that human nature that is not morally tamed is hawkish, one concludes that dovelike behavior is due to serious moral reflection of the kind that seeks to uncover what people could be like if they realized their true telos. This conclusion is stretching Frank's analysis beyond its intended use, but the model opens the door to behavior that may be governed by motives other than pure rational choice self-interest. Perhaps an exploration of the nature of the preferences of cooperator doves is the avenue through which moral reflection can again return to economic analysis. Frank is clear that dove behavior is successful only if it is heartfelt. He argues that cooperative behavior is a choice that, when practiced, becomes part of one's nature. Moral reflection followed by cooperative behavior can lead to actors that have a genuine cooperative nature that does bring preferred outcomes. Frank adds, "By the very nature of the commitment problem, moral sentiments cannot lead to material advantage unless they are heartfelt" (Frank 2010, 233).

People learn, change, and are socialized. They have a spiritual side, which, even if suppressed by enlightenment thinking, does not go away. It identifies with others' needs, it cares about injustice, it seeks what is good in the long run, and it seeks for values grounded in something outside the person. People want to have a telos toward which moral reflection can point, and given the right social institutions, this kind of genuinely cooperative behavior should be able to find expression in other centered behavior. For this reason, it is important that moral reflection is part of the dialogue around which society is formed and modeled.

Herbert Gintis and others have observed that there is a middle ground between purely altruistic behavior and the *homo economicus* maximizer of rational choice economics (Gintis et al. 2005). They draw on a wide range of disciplines including all the social sciences and biology to make the point that economics should be more attuned to how people actually make choices. Gintis and his colleagues conclude that "[E]ffective policies are those that support socially valued outcomes not only by harnessing selfish motives to socially valued ends, but also by evoking, cultivating, and empowering public-spirited motives" (Gintis et al., 4). Much of the middle ground for which the essays argue can be placed in the "tit for tat" strategy of game theory where stable cooperation exists because society develops reliable reciprocal social norms. When agents in a social order realize that a price war in any form will be destructive to everyone, a social norm of reciprocity develops that positions the population for survival better than another group that persists in individual self-interested pursuit such as a damaging price war.

Again, there is no clear line drawn between what is mutually recognized long-term prudent self-interest and what is a genuine other-centered motivation, but the manner in which motives evolve into effective cooperative mechanisms indicates that within a successful society the cooperative motivation can be heartfelt.

Examination of food sharing illustrates how cooperation norms evolve in a social order. In traditional families where food is hunted by a few and shared according to need by all, cooperative norms evolve successfully, but as family connectedness diminishes and common property gives way to private plots, a productivity rewards system is likely to erode the development of heartfelt cooperative behavior (Kaplan and Gurven, 103–104). More research needs to be done in these areas, especially in stranger-to-stranger interaction, in order to better understand just what fosters cooperation, how it is best preserved, and what institutional structure is most amenable to thriving other-centered behavior. Perhaps the least explored area of such behavior is the role played by moral reflection and the spiritual part of one's life.

A subset of cooperative action that has gained traction in economic thinking involves the area of trust. Cooperation works best when people can trust one another, but how is trust developed and practiced? Extensive research by the Russell Sage Foundation on this issue points to the individual, group, and institutional components that foster trust. "Debate exists over whether trust is a feature of the truster, in the form of personality trait, moral commitment or cognitive bias, or a reflection of the trustworthiness of the other, established through a history of interaction, or normative constraints associated with roles occupied by the other person" (Cook et al., 18). While a full review of this literature goes beyond the scope of this chapter, it is instructive to recognize that moral reflection is apparent in the debate at both the individual and institutional level. More needs to be known about how institutions that enhance cooperative behavior are formed, what role moral reflection plays in that formation, and how cooperative behavior is maintained over time.

Is the survival of such institutions dependent on participants who are heartfelt cooperators, or do those institutions foster a cooperative nature in those involved in the system?

Some might argue that some institutions that appear to be based on trust really are driven by competitive self-interest For example, if technology makes credit reports, background checks, or insurance arrangements more readily available or if repeat business is important in transactions, then exchanges that appear to be based on trust may actually involve little trust or risk. We say we trust our banks, not because we know the people in the bank but because the government guarantees our deposits. We trust the government because we know the consequences of defaulting on a promise are severe. These cases stretch the meaning of trust. Simple, rational decision making may also be a factor. However, the ability to acquire information does not necessarily reduce the need for trust.

Despite complex information systems, the financial crisis of 2008–2009 is ample proof that people trusted others in transactions where trust was not merited. One lesson from that experience is that personal integrity and trustworthiness may be increasingly important. Complex technology and low information costs for technologically savvy people may make it harder for rational judgments to substitute for trusting relationships. There is a substantial asymmetry of information where suppliers in a market have much better knowledge of the product than the customer side of the market. The complexity of financial derivatives, medical procedures, and even auto repair has increased the need for interpersonal trust rather than reduced it. Buyers of mortgage-backed securities were not protected by sophisticated technology that helped them make sound purchases. It is becoming increasingly difficult for the average consumer to master the details of complicated consumer goods and services; so trust in supplier integrity is important.

The moral of this story is that personal character traits may well be as important now as they were when friends concluded negotiations or a transaction agreement with a handshake. The quality of moral life significantly affects supply and demand in markets, and trust as a key component of cooperative behavior is likely to increase in importance as complexity advances in social relationships. However, this thesis needs much ongoing study and empirical verification. The fact that data on the moral life is hard to quantify should not deter efforts to integrate it into both theoretical and empirical models.

Beyond the psychological qualifications of economic methodology lies a more mysterious area of study relating to "how the mind works" (Pinker, 1997). This may have a significant long-term impact on how economists work. Using language familiar to economists, Don Ross has proposed a system bringing together the science of the mind with economic preference optimization. Ross writes, "But if the economist therefore admits that she can't rule the world of behavioral explanation alone, evolutionary cognitive science may furnish just the partner she needs to reign as half of a duopoly. For evolutionary cognitive scientists claim to have found a single family of explanatory schemata for handling just those regions the economist can't conquer. That is they will tell us how patterns of preference arise (Pinker, 1997). And they aim to do so using the very logic of optimization, here in the context of evolution's running fitness tournaments, by which the economist lives and breathes" (Ross, 26). Ross believes neurological studies show that the mind is hardwired along self-interest lines with evolutionary competitiveness as the driving force of behavior. In this view, Adam Smith's approach is too wide ranging and folksy in its narrative; moral reflection is unscientific and thus removed from questions economists explore, and much of the interdisciplinary dialogue is limited by a lack of mathematical precision and scientific content. The composition of the brain and its mode of processing will be a frontier of behavioral studies in the years ahead, and the degree of human subjectivity and moral discernment involved will be key variables in the search to uncover how we function.

The field of neuroeconomics is only a decade old, and although professional societies and journals have arisen in the field, there is little consensus yet as to what impact this research will have on economic methodology and its predictions. The simple ultimatum experiment, when conducted with a computer and a human, shows how the brain reacts with moral overtones. In this case, a computer and a human were given $20, and each was told or programmed to distribute a portion of the money to a recipient who then can keep it or return it. If it is returned, the money is lost to both players. Rational choice predicts that any amount will be accepted because, axiomatically, more is preferred to less. Typically, if less than $4 is offered, the receiver will refuse, punishing the person or computer making the one-sided offer. In this experiment, recipients were offended less by low offers from computers than similar offers made by humans, and the result of magnetic resonance imaging (MRI) showed more activity in the insular portion of the brain in the recipients of offers made from humans. This part of the brain relates to negative emotions, so one logical conclusion of this research is that the chemistry of the brain significantly determines what we consider fair or unfair, good or bad (Houser and McCabe, 59). In evaluating the way the brain processes fear, Jon Elster reports that

> [T]here are two different pathways from the sensory apparatus in the thalamus to the amygdala (the part of the brain that causes visceral as well as behavioral emotional responses.) Confirming the traditional view that emotions are always triggered by a cognition, one pathway goes from the thalamus to the neocortex, the thinking part of the brain, and from the

neocortex onward to the amygdala. The organism receives a signal, forms a belief about what it means, and then reacts emotionally. There is also, however, a direct pathway from the thalamus to the amygdala that bypasses the thinking part of the brain entirely.

(Elster, 261–262)

In the first case, emotions are triggered after thinking about the implications, and in the second case, there is an instinctive response that is quicker, as in the case of a sudden confrontation with a poisonous snake. What is interesting about these neurological studies is that, in many cases, the emotional response comes from a place of deliberation that can have moral implications. The emotion of revenge that comes from being offered a small share of the $20 in the ultimatum game presupposes an understanding of justice based on equality. How these emotions are formed and embedded in the brain is not easy to discern, but the moral implications of many emotional reactions point to moral reflection as important in the process.

Because neuroeconomics is in its infancy as a field of study, generalizations from the research findings are tentative at best. After surveying some of the accomplishments of the field, the editors of *Neuroeconomics* suggest that

[D]espite these impressive accomplishments, neuroeconomics is at best a decade old and has yet to demonstrate a critical role in neuroscience, psychology, or economics. Indeed scholars within neuroeconomics are still debating whether neuroscientific data will provide theory for economists or whether economic theory will provide structure for neuroscience. We hope that both goals will be accomplished, but the exact form of this contribution is not yet clear.

(Glimcher et al., 11)

This chapter has only touched on the many ways that economics is being reoriented and stretched to accommodate and consider moral reflection. In many cases, the degree to which traditional rational choice theory is being qualified is uncertain, and there are those who still see the moral concerns as being separated from positive analysis. Nevertheless, ongoing research and discussion should be fruitful exercises as researchers in all the relevant disciplines seek to find a common language and methodology that can expand the frontier of knowledge.

DAN KAHNEMAN: HOW EXPERIENCING COSTS AND BENEFITS DIFFERENTLY ALTERS RATIONAL CHOICE PREDICTIONS

Why would someone refuse a change in a health insurance plan that would lower their premium by $250 and increase the deductable by $200, or why might someone feel worse at the end of the day if their stock portfolio increased in value?

Daniel Kahneman once said that, when he first encountered the rational choice method of analyzing behavior, he had a hard time believing that economists could adopt such a limited approach to human decision making. Stimulated by questions like the ones posed, his research added many insights explaining behavior that seems irrational by economist's standards. For his efforts, he became the first and only psychologist to win a Nobel Prize in Economics, which he was awarded in 2002. In joint work with Amos Tversky, Kahneman found that there are many psychological predispositions that affect how people act. One was the way people put boundaries around their rationality as described in this chapter. Another interesting and applicable finding is that there is asymmetry in how we count gains and losses. To answer the preceding questions about health insurance and stock portfolios, see Figure 8.1.

Rational choice would say that if you gain $250 in premium reduction and cannot lose more than $200 in additional health care expenses you would take the new offer from your employer. However, as the figure illustrates, your utility is reduced by 150 if you must pay an extra $200 of your expenses, but your utility is increased only by 100 when your income rises by $250 due to the reduced insurance premium. This asymmetry in utility functions may be surprising, but what is more unusual is the fact that people separate the gains and losses as two separate events when they consider the policy change. Given the option to switch to the plan with these new features, it would be logical to consider the difference of $50 and recognize that it will increase overall welfare. Yet many refused to switch (Frank, 241). This finding has many applications. At the end of a day when one of your stocks has gained $110 in value and another has lost $100, you may feel worse, but there is no apparent reason why you would separate the events rather than look at the balance at the end of the day. Our minds do not always follow

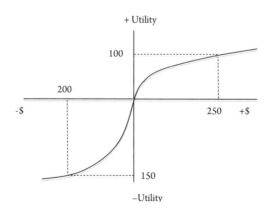

Figure 8.1 Asymmetric Value Functions

the logical rational choice patterns, and so behavior may frequently be unpredictable when using standard economic analysis. In many ways, Kahneman has opened the door to creative interdisciplinary research that enriches and broadens the scope of economic analysis.

Questions for Discussion

1. Which would make you feel best of the following two scenarios? All points have equal weight. a) Ten weekly 10-point quiz scores of 9.5 each and a score of 75 on a 100-point exam. b) All quiz and exam scores of 85. Does your answer fit with Kahneman's asymmetric value functions?
2. Use the graph to explain why credit cards are so popular with retailers.
3. Does the asymmetric value function explain why car dealers offer rebates instead of lower prices?
4. Can you think of other ways that psychology impacts behavior in ways that rational choice does not predict? To find other interesting examples, do an Internet search for Daniel Kahneman and find other applications.

WHY DO MARKETS NEVER STAND ALONE? AMARTYA SEN, FAMINES, AND POSITIVE FREEDOM

Can economics help us understand human suffering? Millions of people starve due to droughts, flooding, natural catastrophes like earthquakes or tsunamis, or human food distribution mechanisms that operate inequitably. If crops are largely wiped out or rot in warehouses, and famines result in sub-Saharan Africa or the sub-continent of India, can markets be relied upon to address famines as many economists claim?

The 1998 Nobel Prize–winner Amartya Sen's spent his life exploring these questions. Growing up in prepartition India in West Bengal, at an early age Sen saw firsthand the ravaging effects of the 1943 Bengal famine. His work in development and welfare economics has been shaped by an understanding of the realities of human suffering and the role economic institutions play in either ameliorating or exacerbating such suffering. Sen's brightest contribution to economic policy centers on the notion of understanding human freedom positively, in terms of capabilities that are nurtured by the proper institutions. These "capacities" are human abilities that can flourish when barriers related to racial and ethnic class or education are removed, and access to credit, medicine, and food are improved. When people are impoverished, they lack the capability to function at a minimal level, often due to the lack of freedoms presented by institutional barriers.

So how has the application of these concepts contributed to economists' understanding of famines? Sen's research on the pattern of famines points him to the key role that ancillary factors supporting or hindering market mechanisms play in causing and alleviating widespread starvation. Examining the pattern of famines in India, Ethiopia and the Sahel, and China, Sen finds that most often total food output during years of famines does not lag behind nonfamine annual food output. Thus he affirms "Starvation is the characteristic of some people not having enough food to eat. It is not the characteristic of there being not enough food to eat" (Sen 1982, 1). Urban ethnic and racial minorities starve when food distribution mechanisms are unfair, as when they are grounded in racial or class discrimination. Farm laborers starve when the purchasing power of their income fails to keep pace with rising food prices, not because there are too many stomachs related to food supply. Nations can experience famines even when "the ratio of food to population (on which Malthus concentrated) goes up rather than down" (Dreze and Sen 1989, 25).

Sen recognizes that markets have a key function in alleviating suffering by providing incentives through rising prices to bring forth greater food supply, a claim made by Adam Smith in his discussion of the proper public policy approach to famines. Suppression of trade in food output through price controls only exacerbates starvation. Yet Sen states that Smith would not have opposed market activity being supplemented by selective government intervention to create purchasing power "for the disentitled population" when combined with a policy of leaving "the supply of food to respond to the newly created demand through private trade" (Dreze and Sen 1995, 54). Beyond episodic governmental provision of income supplements, Sen proclaims the need for other institutions to supplement the market such as a free media and a functioning democracy. A multiplicity of voices needs to be heard, including those bearing economic grievances with barriers that hinder their enjoyment of positive economic freedom, and governments must be held accountable to the demands of the electorate. In this regard, Sen has famously observed that no famine has ever occurred in a country with a free press and regular elections.

Thus for Sen, markets never stand alone. Desirable social policy promotes greater access to participation in markets through greater availability of education, training, and credit. These kinds of considerations have driven Sen to be heavily involved in fashioning better measures of human economic progress, such as the human development index produced for the United Nations Development Program. Instead of relying solely on macroeconomic criteria such as national income, savings rates, and gross domestic product (GDP) growth rates, this measure emphasizes a nation's performance with respect to life expectancy, education, and adult literacy rates. Sen's focus, then, is not so much on material welfare standards as on the ways material products foster human ingenuity. Human development occurs when institutions provide people with the freedom they need to reach their potential.

Questions for Discussion

1. Looking at the last half of the twentieth century, how does the lack of famine in democratic India stand in contrast with China's experience during its Great Leap Forward? How would you explain the difference in the two nation's performance with respect to human starvation using Sen's reasoning?

2. What types of barriers to human capacity still exist for lower-income individuals in the United States? How might they be removed?

3. What specific social and economic indicators should be included in any robust measure of a nation's development? Explain in terms of the significance of its citizens' capabilities.

Chapter 9

Predicting, Explaining, and Understanding

An Interdisciplinary Approach

So far we have traced the way moral reflection influenced economic thinking and life in ancient and medieval times and noted that, when science took over as the methodological framework in the Enlightenment period, moral thinking factored less centrally in economic decision making. We then examined numerous critiques of the modern rational choice approach to economics and explored some of the present efforts to go beyond the instrumentalist objectives predominant in mainstream economics today. In most cases, the concerns of the critics focus on the limited objectives of economics as a science. Predicting behavior as a goal that trumps all other objectives feels inadequate to many. There is a desire to incorporate an understanding of behavior and to explore why people do what they do. Everyone is aware that we do not act as individual entities and that maximizing personal pleasure, as it is construed in economic theory, does not describe how we live much of our lives. Although freedom is high on our list of values, we also seek boundaries and constraints that help us define who we are and what we ought to do. Isolating aspects of behavior and influence into specialties may make research less cluttered, but it leaves much of our story untold.

What follows is an attempt to sketch a framework for how a sociopolitical economy might enrich the way we understand our economic decisions. Economics can be more than the mechanistic theoretical framework of neoclassical micro and macro theory as we know it. Any sociopolitical economy should begin with an assessment of the human passions and instincts that are operative and the interpersonal and institutional structures that socialize those passions. Then the compatibility of the institutional structures must be considered. One of the problems in the current dialogue about whether rational choice best describes our behavior or whether some other passions are operative is that there is often little discussion about the social context involved. One way to approach this problem is to list the various contexts in which we operate and then explore the nature of the relationships involved in each context. Institutionalists of various kinds have done this sort of exploration with some success, but in many cases the analysis ends with rational choice assumptions whether the context is the family, the church, the neighborhood, or the nation. Figure 9.1 illustrates this issue.

When social scientists analyze human behavior with rational choice methods, they tend to treat all of the relationships represented in figure 9.1 as governed by the same motivations. Yet many of these circles operate by motivations other than narrow self-regard. People living in a healthy family situation will often give up personal preferences to accommodate the wishes of other family members because love and caring are the motivating forces driving behavior. Close friends operate from reciprocity rather than self-interest, and other social norms based on egalitarian sentiments often regulate relationships in ways that rational choice cannot predict. Those involved in a church fellowship look to values beyond themselves, frequently engaging in altruistic activity that contrasts sharply with rational choice motivation. The same is true for many civic organizations and social groups that are formed to address a cause larger than

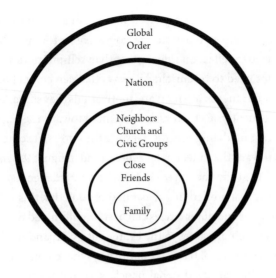

Figure 9.1 Relationships in the social order

narrow self-interest. Funding for these organizations comes largely from voluntary contributions, and there is no effort to coerce people into compliance with the expectations of the group because no one is forced to join the cause. In most cases, the benefits from group participation can be restricted to those who are committed to the group cause and who contribute their fair share. Neighbors in a healthy community operate out of a sense of fairness recognizing the common good that can come from mutual respect. This attitude must be heartfelt, or the opportunities to forgo the group mentality for personal gain will sooner or later destroy neighborhood solidarity.

So far, rational choice will be able to predict behavior accurately only when the social group becomes dysfunctional. Families fall apart, friendships fail, churches spiritualize their mission and ignore temporal human concerns, and neighborhoods frequently experience tension when some pursue their self-interest. Rational choice may be of instrumental use in these cases, but it will fail to predict with accuracy when the preferred motivations are practiced. The preceding examples illustrate the complexity of human behavior and the need to reflect on values other than self-promotion. Models of behavior need to be enriched in ways that can compel people to reflect on the range of instincts and motivations they share. Yet economists frequently see their task as oriented toward the impersonal and abstract modeling process. Despite the efforts of some to push analysis toward the inner circles represented in figure 9.1, most find it fruitful to study the outer circles where interdependence is less apparent. It is an underlying thesis of this book that this separation between inner and outer circles can best be eliminated not by pushing the outer circle values to the center but by expanding the inner circle values outward. If this is done in ways that complement rather than compete with traditional neoclassical modeling, economics will speak to a broader audience and foster a meaningful discussion of what people really want and what is good for people individually and collectively. Moral reflection will become part of the social process because the formation of individual choices in the impersonal world will be influenced by the kinds of relationships experienced in daily life where the moral dimension is operative.

The state, national, global, and to some extent local communities operate with a different set of values than the idealized inner-circle relationships. In the public sphere, participation is mandatory because the goods provided fit the public good category. People cannot be excluded from the good or service once it is provided, and if another person joins the community the quantity of the good produced or service provided does not need to be increased. There is also little direct interaction among the citizens, and reaping benefits without contributing is easy unless there is some form of coercion compelling people to contribute their share. Consequently, taxes are mandatory and, in cases where public provision is in the form of insurance, everyone is required to join the insurance pool to avoid the adverse selection problem. In this circle of impersonal relation-ships, rational choice analysis tends to work well because people are expected to follow their own interests given the constraints of the social order. Good policy will structure the rules in ways that chan-nel behavior toward the desired outcome.

In the private sector outer circles, the market is the allocator of resources, and it plays an essential role in coordinating activity that is impersonal. Market prices are the key signals to which people respond, and so the maximization of individual utility is operative in ways that make rational choice predictions reliable in most cases. Mainstream economic theory presumes that moral reflection is not relevant in these settings. Unfortunately, this claim ignores the moral context of markets, and the fact that behavior in the outer circles requires a level of personal integrity and trust that cannot be taken for granted. Daniel Friedman, in *Morals and Markets,* explores the connection between the two. Recognizing that there is a tension between what we have termed inner and outer circles, Friedman claims that "[H]umans evolved two distinctive new ways to cope with this dilemma. Morals go back to our human origins, and work best in small groups. Markets work best at large scale, and their rise 200 years ago ushered in the modern world. With 6.6 billion mouths to feed, divorce is not an option. Prospects for the future will brighten when reformers, and the general public, bet-ter understand the marriage of morals and markets and work to improve it" (Friedman, 4). Attempts to divorce the two with a posi-tive/normative methodology understate the role of moral reflection needed in all the circles of the social order. Outcomes of market activity will vary greatly depending on what values are operative in the social system.

As the scope of the relationships widen beyond the national economy to global markets, there is no overarching mechanism for coerced participation where public goods are involved, nor does a common set of values regulate market behavior. People do not see global causes superseding national interests so international relationships are frequently successfully modeled with rational choice assumptions or with game theoretic models that operate from inwardly motivated behavior. Supranational institutions such as the World Trade Organization, the World Bank, the International Monetary Fund, and the United Nations were formed to harmonize the world order, but divergent values make common worldwide practices difficult.

The farther from the center of the concentric circles one goes, the more fruitful rational choice analysis will be, but nowhere across the social order can moral reflection be ignored. How, one might ask, can rational choice methods be successfully used to predict behavior in some of the inner circles of figure 9.1? Successful prediction could occur because both an outward and inward orientation in some cases might result in the same behavior or because the idealized models of family, friends, church, and civic group do not exist. Families have become dysfunctional, churches have sometimes preached a gospel that contains mainly private benefits, and friendships and civic groups involve many who seek private benefit or public stature from their social connections. For these reasons, rational choice leads to mixed results when the inner circles are considered.

All of this discussion about figure 9.1 is to make a simple point. Proponents of rational choice methods and critics of its use frequently are talking past one another because one group is focusing on the outer circles and the other group is focusing on the idealized inner circles. The attractiveness of the inner-circle relationships relates to the desire people have for more intimacy and a values-driven life. Love, caring, and socially responsible activity are appealing, and when they are stripped from the way we see human interactions, there is a resulting void that makes value-free methodology seem harsh whether or not it predicts adequately.

In order to observe economic life in its larger context, we need to see behavior as driven by our basic instincts, the social context, the existing institutional structures, and the values embedded in our world-view. For example, if we assume that the passion of revenge is best dealt with by the political institutions of lawmaking and law enforcing, and if we assume that the acquisitive passions are best moderated by the institution of the marketplace, then it is important that the market and the political institutions we promote be compatible and fit the values we hold. If they are not, social cohesion will be limited and the social order precarious.

One of the difficulties in exploring behavior exclusively through the lens of rational choice is that we live in many different contexts and each one operates with its own set of expectations and norms as described in figure 9.1. Daniel Bell, in *The Cultural Contradictions of Capitalism*, examines incompatibilities that exist among the economic, social, and cultural milieus of modern capitalist societies (Bell 1976). The call for patriotic unity seems inconsistent with the claim that we are all individualists in the marketplace. On Sunday in church, many are encouraged to look after those less fortunate, and on Monday we are told to seek our own interests and everyone will be better off in the end. We all fill many different roles in life, and we have a deep need to see ourselves as an integrated, whole person with some useful purpose. All of these efforts point to a comprehensive social-cultural-political-economic-moral perspective, which we are calling a social-political economy. It should be an interdisciplinary complement to rather than a substitute for discipline-specific methods, and the claim is that neither approach by itself is sufficient. Each method leans on its counterpart for balance with the objective being a more holistic understanding of human behavior and better predictions of what we will do.

Accordingly, this approach starts from the innate passions of humanity as delineated by Adam Smith and David Hume and couples it with the human instincts articulated by Thorstein Veblen and other institutionalist economists. Veblen's paternal instinct has similar qualities to his workmanship instinct discussed in chapter 6. It arose from the caring for basic resources in ancient times; so it carries over to modern times as an outward attitude that includes a concern for others. Smith and Veblen had vastly differing approaches to economics, but each began by examining the nature of the person. There are similarities in how they diagnosed human nature, even though they proposed decidedly different strategies for how that nature would best be socialized and fulfilled. The last category in table 9.1 is enlarged beyond the intent of either Smith or Veblen to include that part of our makeup that deals with spiritual consciousness and beliefs that seem to be a part of every culture no matter how developed they become. These need not be religious, but they often are part of religious beliefs and practices.

Thus the search for enduring social cohesion becomes inter-disciplinary as we recognize that there may need to be trade-offs among the differing social institutions. No one institutional struc-ture like the market or the polity can optimize solely within its own domain. Table 9.1 shows a matrix approach to social-political econ-omy. First, four categories are presented that incorporate both the passions and instincts of Smith and Veblen. Then the social sphere of action is listed for each category. The third column illustrates the social institution that is most involved in containing or organizing the respective passions. Finally, a column of possible issues that would come under each category is shown. This chart will become the basis from which a social-political economy will be discussed.

To consider human activity along only one row may simplify analysis, but it will ignore important considerations. To ignore any row is to impoverish the social-political economy. For example, suppose the economic sphere reaches optimal efficiency with a highly advanced technological base, but to prevent technological

Table 9.1 A SOCIOPOLITICAL FRAMEWORK

Human Passions	Sphere of Action	Governing Structure	Issues
Veblen's acquisitive and workmanship instincts & Smith's selfish passions of pain/pleasure choices and self preservation.	Economy	Market	GDP, individual freedom, competition, exchange
Smith's unsocial passions of hate, envy and revenge. Veblen's paternal instinct.	Polity	Government or State	Public goods, rule of law protecting individual rights, merit goods
Smith's social passions of esteem and desire for approval and Veblen's paternal instinct	Society	Numerous communities like family, neighborhood, church, town, nation	Social identity, recognition, security, shared values, maintaining particularism
Smiths social passions of generosity and compassion. Veblen' idle curiosity instinct.	Religion	Church etc. and impartial spectator	Inner spiritual longings, the need to serve

189

sabotage and to protect technical property rights the political sphere must become more authoritarian. In this situation, a proper balance between efficiency and political interference cannot be reached apart from interdisciplinary discourse. In the days following the September 11, 2001, terrorist attacks the sense of national unity and sacrifice led to behavior that could not have been accurately predicted by rational choice methods. The same was true after Hurricane Katrina hit New Orleans. When bonuses were given to employees of failing companies such as AIG and Merrill Lynch, the public did not admire the rational self-interested skills of those who obtained the lucrative contracts. Rather, the outcry of injustice condemned the behavior as deplorable, not just because public money was expended to help the firms stay solvent, but because some would profit despite poor performance when many productive citizens were suffering from hard times. Social solidarity, fairness, and justice in these cases become boundaries within which rational choice behavior must operate for such behavior to be seen as rational in the long run. Consequently a dialogue between social, political, and ethical considerations must take place before any meaningful optimization process can exist across the economic row in table 9.1.

A reasonable rejoinder to these examples is that they are exceptional cases where extreme circumstances existed and, while rational choice may fail to predict behavior in such cases, it still is the tool of choice in most normal situations. This argument is hard to prove or disprove, although it is fairly clear that rationality always has some boundaries so the issue becomes identifying which boundaries are relevant and how restrictive they are. One theme of this book is that the moral, political, and social boundaries of the social system are intertwined and need to be analyzed more holistically when models of human behavior are constructed.

This is not to suggest that analysis along any row cannot be helpful. An econometric analysis of data on a topic can provide insights that need to become part of the total picture being observed. However, in practice economists may rely solely on the quantitative measures. As McCloskey argues in regard to the fetish economists have with statistical analysis, "They are left...with a senseless rhetoric of quantification: the 'statistical test of significance.' It is the consequence of not asking 'How large is large?' Something has gone very wrong with the quantitative rhetoric of economics" (McCloskey 1998, 11).

The question of how large is large can only be determined through considered dialogue that occurs within the political framework of public choice, the social norms and values that exist in a given culture, and the spiritual beliefs that impact the society. Nevertheless, one might still argue that this is all true, but social scientists as specialists still work within the framework of their respective disciplines and then some more generalized social process must blend the information. In this view, the economist provides a theoretical model and statistical coefficients for use by others who then bring together the political, social, and values-oriented concerns into some workable policy.

There are two problems with this approach of the economist as specialist. First, it overlooks the nature of data itself. Data has a context and rarely escapes interpretive screens and biases that can only be recognized when viewed across all rows of analysis. For example, the GDP per capita of a particular nation is often used as a measure of comparative welfare among various economies. Yet cultural and social norms frequently vary so that some countries do far more market exchanges than others. A culture where much economic activity is done outside of measurable market exchanges will look much worse in comparison to a modern economy where nearly all goods and services pass through a market. Some estimate of the size of the underground economy is necessary to make the GDP per capita variable meaningful, and an understanding of the sociological context will be required to have a good feel for the extent of nonmarket economic activity. Furthermore, some psychological benefit might derive from being self-sufficient, and bartering can be more meaningful than the larger market exchanges that tend to be much more impersonal. Databases will frequently overlook these social and psychological aspects of the issue being studied. This is not to say that databases economists use lack social and psychological input. The claim here is that such input tends to make the data less precise while it adds more understanding to behavior. There are trade-offs in the process of predicting, explaining, and understanding.

A second reason why economists need an interdisciplinary perspective involves the concept of the second best. The economist as specialist adopts a "more is preferred to less" assumption that is built into rational choice thinking. For example, suppose a home buyer is seeking a house with a half-acre lot as the optimal choice. When none is available it is assumed that a slightly smaller one will do. However, if having the largest lot has significant social meaning, a smaller lot may be rejected in favor of a penthouse condominium. In other words, the second-best option is something totally different from a slightly reduced amount of the optimum choice. Incremental analysis of variables in economic models will fail to pick up these discontinuities created by social norms or psychological preferences.

A neoclassical theorist will agree that behavior is far more complex than utility-maximizing models allow, but she assumes that the social, political, and values concerns can be attached to the analysis by the policy specialists. However, a more likely case is that the best problem solving will arise from an integrated theory rather than from piecing together of specialized discipline analysis. A proper conception of social economics will integrate a theory of human behavior with a theory of empirical reality in such a way that the policy can speak to the most fundamental needs of humanity.

It might be argued that economists are increasingly considering the four spheres of action in their analysis and that methodological adjustments are well under way. The last chapter illustrated many areas where traditional analysis is being augmented. Examples of economists moving in this direction include forays into topics such as addiction, positional goods, stigma and discrimination, abortion, bounded rationality, trust, fairness, commitment devices, and principle-agent issues. The religious and social needs of individuals are also sometimes incorporated into individual utility functions in ways that attempt to avoid a present-aim rationality approach. One might also point to the manner in which the new institutionalists are exploring the role of institutions such as property rights in the social order. All of these practices show that mainstream economists are increasingly aware of the narrowness of their methodology, but these efforts to broaden the scope of analysis often do not get at the core of the problem because they frequently fail to escape the rational choice framework. What results is an economic imperialism that bends all the social sciences toward an analysis of only the acquisitive and self-serving passions and instincts.

This focus on one set of passions and instincts has robbed social analysis of one of its most important initiatives, but it might also have embedded within itself the seeds of its own destruction. Charles L. Griswold Jr. poses this problem:

> Might the apparent devolution of liberty into spontaneity, of pluralism into relativism, of knowledge into technology and thence into the self-vitiating mastery of nature, of science into a worldview produced by a given historical milieu, of culture into vulgarity, of reason into imagination and then into fantasy—in

short the devolution of the Enlightenment into what is widely termed 'postmodernism'—itself be a natural consequence of the very premises of the Enlightenment?

(Griswold 3)

One might add that the notion of the specialization of labor has spread into academic disciplines that become compartmentalized, unified only by a common methodology of rational choice.

Griswold's argument might be used by some to show that the contextual, social, and moral categories described in this book are examples of a move away from the truth- seeking that characterizes scientific methods as it searches for secure foundations. On the contrary, it is the effort to reduce the whole person to *homo economicus* that has separated social analysis from the way life is experienced and that disconnection leads to the concerns Griswold raises. A premise of this chapter is that methods contributing to a fuller picture of human behavior will likely be more effective than a one-dimensional caricature of economic life at preventing what Griswold calls a drift to postmodernism. In addition to the efforts being made in social, psychological, and biological areas, it is important to recognize than an internal moral compass still exists in humans as a necessary component of our collective existence.

It is a contention of this book that if the Enlightenment had built on Adam Smith's concept of a naturalistic, interdisciplinary moral system rather than been diverted into a mechanistic, value-free scientific enterprise, modern economics might not have acquired such a narrow focus. Of course what we would have might be as subjective and contextual as moral sympathy, and moral understanding might be as ambiguous as the impartial spectator. However, reality as interpretation, understanding as contextual, and belief as commitment would seem less frightening if they were framed in a context of a naturalized moral system.

The appeal of Smith's approach is that both moral sympathy and the impartial spectator protected individual autonomy while relying on existing norms, social expectations, and circumstances. Both Smith and Veblen recognized this interdependence and the role of emotion in human behavior. They saw the subjective nature of social analysis and were not enslaved by a contrived fact-value dichotomy. Both moved freely across the landscape of the four categories in the preceding chart and they were more interested in the search for contextual workable principles than for some absolute truth in the science of economics. While Smith sought the natural tendencies extant in society, he did not see those tendencies being worked out within some proven system of abstract social laws or from philosophical reasoning. Rather, what was natural was what was convincing to the casual but thoughtful observer from the emotions or passions that were common to everyone. Thus moral and economic principles of the social order were formed from innate instincts and emotions expressed in a social context.

While it is less clear where Veblen's instincts originate from, the interplay of the contrasting instincts takes place within and is conditioned by the existing institutional patterns. This interplay is essentially between the three socially desirable instincts, on the one hand, and the unsocial instincts of acquisitiveness and greed on the other hand. Veblen referred to this tension as a dichotomy from which evolved social structures and norms. Veblen and Smith differ in their approach to system building. Smith is trying to fit the pieces of the social process together into a unified system while Veblen's approach is the antithesis of any system-building project. For Veblen, the flow of events and institutions is so subject to change that a highly structured predictable system is likely to be of limited value.

It is important to keep in mind that the purpose of this book is to put moral reflection into the formula for applying economics and analyzing social systems. In practice, economic systems are infused with ethical and moral concerns, and everyone operates with some type of value system that guides economic activity. Deirdre McCloskey makes this point forcefully in the *Bourgeois Virtues*. Working from the thesis that all of the classical virtues are operative in the market economy when it is functioning properly, she illustrates that markets are deficient when its virtues are out of balance, as occurred during the Enlightenment when prudence was elevated to an exclusive position in markets to the detriment of other virtues. Many of the virtues McCloskey describes would fit with the passions and instincts of Smith and Veblen and therefore help to flesh out the grid of economic thinking that this chapter is advancing. Behavior has many dimensions requiring a multi-faceted approach to predicting, explaining, and understanding. Without a fuller account of action than rational choice offers, the ethical and moral components of living will be underplayed if not ignored.

Donald Frey examines the role of moral reflection in economic thinking throughout the history of the United States, claiming that two strains of thought drove markets. Autonomy morality and relational morality are categories that fit U.S. history with autonomy morality dominating the scene from the Enlightenment period onward. In many ways, both McCloskey and Frey complement each other in their work because Frey's thesis about autonomy fits with McCloskey's argument that prudence-driven markets will leave them deficient. Both authors find markets to be enriched by a full range of ethical input that comes from moral, philosophical, psychological, and historical reflection.

Piecemeal analysis may be mathematically neat, give the appearance of vigor, and offer selective insights into what we might do in various situations, but it cannot capture the imagination in ways that the fuller story of an actual life is capable of doing. There is no

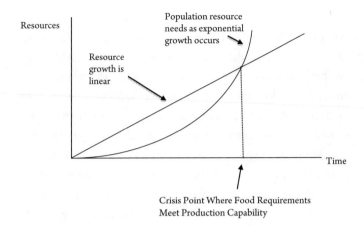

Figure 9.2 Thomas Malthus and Resource Exhaustion

substitute for moral reflection, and without it, there is a void in how we think about ourselves and what we do.

THOMAS MALTHUS: IS THE WORLD RUNNING OUT OF RESOURCES?

As the eighteenth century was drawing to a close, there was an ongoing debate about whether economic growth could improve the lives of everyone. Yet there was one limiting factor that seemed hard to control. Population increases move in geometric fashion creating an exponential growth curve that will outstrip any efforts to increase the food supply that does not grow exponentially as well. Graphically the dilemma can be represented by showing food increasing in a linear fashion but population multiplying geometrically as shown in Figure 9.2.

In Malthus's words, "It has been said that the great question is now at issue, whether man shall henceforth start forward with accelerated velocity towards illimitable, and hitherto unconceived improvement, or be condemned to a perpetual oscillation between happiness and misery, and after every effort remain still at an immeasurable distance from the wished-for-goal" (Malthus, 16).

Some, such as William Godwin, argued that people could learn to control reproductive passions and that would lower the population's need for resources, thereby raising the average standard of living. Malthus, however, was more pessimistic, believing that people would take the initial increase in living standards as an opportunity to have larger families, thus fostering faster population growth. Sexual passions dominated the required discipline needed to control population. Therefore, society will quickly move to the crisis point beyond which only war, pestilence, and famine could keep population in check. Subsistence living would inevitably be the lot of society. For Malthus, voluntary efforts to restrict population, which he called preventive checks, will fail, and the positive checks of subsistence living will bring great distress and hardship to families. Malthus further prophesied that "[T]o these two great checks to population ... may be added vicious customs with respect to women, great cities, unwholesome manufactures, luxury, pestilence, and war. All these checks may be fairly resolved into misery and vice" (Malthus, 44).

Throughout the early part of the nineteenth century, this pessimistic Malthusian doctrine carried great weight in social thought, and the Malthusian hypothesis is still debated today as the world population grows and resources such as energy and food are stretched. Only a small portion of the world matches the U.S. standard of living, which has been maintained to some degree by borrowing from various other nations for the last few decades. Now with energy shortages and environmental concerns pressing the world economy, the production line in the graph may not reach the level hoped for over time (unless human ingenuity raises productivity sufficiently through the application of technological innovation). This will hasten the crisis point and bring Malthusian thinking back into the public dialogue.

Questions for Discussion

1. Economic growth in the United States and Europe has lowered population growth rates dramatically as families choose two jobs and a higher standard of living over large families. Is this likely to happen in places such as India and China as growth occurs?

2. What is your opinion of family-size limitations enforced or strongly encouraged by governments as has been the case in China?

3. Malthus lists large cities and the luxuries of a few as being part of the misery and vice he sees. Do you see the urbanization movement and more unequal distribution of income as leading to vice and misery?

4. Malthus felt that the Poor Laws, which provided some money for the indigent, would lead to bigger families and continued poverty. Is this view of family size relevant today, and if so, are there any moral considerations that might qualify such a position?

5. The nineteenth and twentieth centuries have brought about substantial growth in production, and technological change has substantially raised the world's production capacity. Do you see new technologies rescuing the world from energy and environmental disasters now and in the future, or do you have a more Malthusian approach to what lies ahead in the twenty-first century?

BIBLIOGRAPHY

Adler, Mortimer J. (1979). *Aristotle for Everyone*. New York: Macmillan.

Allen, Robert C. (2009). *The British Industrial Revolution in Global Perspective*. Cambridge: Cambridge University Press.

Aquinas, Thomas. (1981 [1365]). *Summa Theologica*. 5 vols. Westminster, MD: Christian Classics.

Aristotle (1954). *Politics*. Trans. Benjamin Jowett. In *Source Readings in Economic Thought*, P. Newman, A. D. Gayer, and M. H. Spencer, eds. New York: Norton, 6–14.

Aristotle (1996). *Nicomachean Ethics*. Trans. Harris Rackham. Hertfordshire, UK: Wadsworth.

Backhouse, Roger E. (1997). *Truth and Progress in Economic Knowledge*. Cheltenham: UK, Edward Elgar.

Backhouse, Roger E. (2010). *The Puzzle of Modern Economics*. Cambridge UK: Cambridge University Press.

Barrotta, Pierluigi (2008). "Why Economists Should Be Unhappy with the Economics of Happiness." *Journal of Economics and Philosophy* 2:145–165.

Bauer, Peter (2000). *From Subsistence to Exchange*. Princeton, NJ: Princeton University Press.

Becker, Gary S. (1993). *A Treatise on the Family*. Cambridge, MA: Harvard University Press.

Beckerman, Wilfred (2011). *Economics as Applied Ethics: Value Judgments in Welfare Economics*. New York: Palgrave MacMillan.

Bell, Daniel (1976). *Cultural Contradictions of Capitalism*. New York: Basic Books.

Bentham, Jeremy (1954 [1789]). *An Introduction to the Principles of Morals and Legislation*. In *Source Readings in Economic Thought*, P. Newman, A. D. Gayer, and M. H. Spencer, eds. New York:, 165–169.

Bible. (2008). *The English Standard Version*. Wheaton, IL: Crossway.

Binmore, Ken (2009). *Rational Decisions*. Princeton, NJ: Princeton University Press.

Blaug, Mark (1996). *Economic Theory in Retrospect*. 5th ed., Cambridge: Cambridge University Press.

Boettke, Peter J. (2010). "Back to the Future: Austrian Economics in the Twenty-First Century." In *Handbook of Contemporary Austrian Economics*, Peter J. Boettke, ed. Cheltenham, UK: Edward Elgar.

Bonanno, Giacomo, et. al. (2008). *Economics and Philosophy* 24 (3) (November), special issue on neuroeconomics. Cambridge, UK: Cambridge University Press.

Brown, Vivienne (1991). "Signifying Voices: Reading the 'Adam Smith Problem.'" *Journal of Economics and Philosophy* 2:187–220.

Buchan, James (2006). *The Authentic Adam Smith*. New York: Atlas Books.

Buchanan, James M. (1975). *The Limits to Liberty: Between Anarchy and Leviathan*. Chicago: University of Chicago Press.

Burtt, Everett Johnson, Jr. (1972). *Social Perspectives in the History of Economic Theory*. New York: St. Martins Press.

Busch, Lawrence, (2000). *The Eclipse of Morality: Science, State and Market*. New York: Aldine De Gruyter.

Butler, Eamonn (1985). *Hayek: His Contribution to the Political and Economic Thought of Our Time*. New York: Universe Books.

Caldwell, Bruce (1994). *Beyond Positivism: Economic Methodology in the Twentieth Century*. London: Routledge.

Caldwell, Bruce (2004). *Hayek's Challenge: An Intellectual Biography of F. A. Hayek*. Chicago: University of Chicago Press.

Carruthers, Bruce G. (2009). "Trust and Credit." In *Whom Can We Trust*, K. Cook, M. Levi, and R Hardin, eds. New York: Russell Sage Foundation.

Castells, Manuel (1996). *The Rise of the Network Society*. Oxford: Blackwell.

Clark, Barry (1998). *Political Economy: A Comparative Approach*. 2nd ed. Westport, CT: Praeger.

Coase, Ronald (1975). "Adam Smith's View of Man." *Journal of Law and Economics* 19:529–546.

Colander, David, Richard P. F. Holt, and J. Barkley Rosser Jr., eds. (2007). *The Changing Face of Economics: Conversations with Cutting Edge Economists*. Ann Arbor: University of Michigan Press.

Conway, David (1987). *A Farewell to Marx: An Outline and Appraisal of His Theories*. New York: Penguin Books.

Cook, K., M. Levi, and R. Hardin, eds. (2009). *Whom Can We Trust*. New York: Russell Sage Foundation.

Cropsey, Joseph (2001). *Polity and Economy*. South Bend, IN: St. Augustine's Press.

Demsetz, Harold (2008). *From Economic Man to Economic System: Essays on Human Behavior and the Institutions of Capitalism*. Cambridge: Cambridge University Press.

Diggins, John P. (1999). *Thorstein Veblen: Theorist of the Leisure Class*. Princeton, NJ: Princeton University Press.

Dreze, J., and Amartya K. Sen (1989). *Hunger and Public Action*. Oxford: Clarendon Press.

Dreze, J. and Amartya K. Sen (1995). *India: Economic Development and Social Opportunity*. Oxford: Oxford University Press.

Easterlin, Richard A. (2000). "The Worldwide Standard of Living since 1800." *Journal of Economic Perspectives* 14:7–26.

Easterlin, Richard A. (2010). *Happiness, Growth, and the Life Cycle*. Ed. Holger Hinte and Klaus F. Zimmermann. New York, Oxford University Press.

Edgell, Stephen (2001). *Veblen in Perspective: His Life and Thought*. Armonk, NY:, M. E. Sharpe.

Elster, Jon (2007). *Explaining Social Behavior: More Nuts and Bolts for the Social Scientists*. Cambridge: Cambridge University Press.

Evensky, Jerry (2007). *Adam Smith's Moral Philosophy: A Historical and Contemporary Perspective on Markets, Law, Ethics, and Culture*. Cambridge: Cambridge University Press.

Fleischacker, Samuel (2004). *On Adam Smith's Wealth of Nations, A Philosophical Companion*, Princeton, NJ: Princeton University Press.

Foddy, Margaret, and Toshio Yamagishi (2009). "Group Based Trust." In *Whom Can We Trust*, K. Cook, M. Levi, and R. Hardin, eds. New York: Russell Sage Foundation.

Frank, Robert H. (1988). *Passions within Reason*. New York: Norton.

Frank, Robert H. (2010). *Microeconomics and Behavior*. New York: McGraw-Hill.

Frey, Bruno S. (2008). *Happiness: A Revolution in Economics*. Cambridge, MA: MIT Press.

Frey, Donald (2009). *America's Economic Moralists*. Albany: State University of New York Press.

Friedman, Daniel (2008). *Morals and Markets*. New York: Palgrave Macmillan.

Friedman, Milton, (1953). *Essays in Positive Economics*. Chicago: University of Chicago Press.

Fullbrook, Edward, ed. (2004). *A Guide to What Is Wrong with Economics*. London: Anthem Press.

Gintis, H., S. Bowles, R. Boyd, and E. Fehr (2005). "Moral Sentiments and Material Interests: Origins, Evidence, and Consequences." In *Moral*

Sentiments and Material Interests, H. Gintis, S. Bowles, R. Boyd, and E. Fehr, eds. Cambridge, MA: MIT Press.

Glimcher, P., C. Camerer, E. Fehr, and R. Poldrack, eds. (2009). *Neuroeconomics: Decision Making and the Brain*. Amsterdam: Academic Press.

Gordon, Barry (1963) "Aristotle and Hesiod: The Economic Problem in Greek Thought." Reprinted in Rima, Ingrid H. (1970) *Readings in the History of Economic Theory*, New York: Holt, Rinehardt and Winston.

Gordon, Barry. (1975). *Economic Analysis before Adam Smith: Hesiod to Lessius*. London: Macmillan.

Gotthelf, Allan (2000). *On Ayn Rand*. Belmont, CA: Wadsworth.

Gould, Stephen J. (1980). *The Panda's Thumb: More Reflections on Natural History*. New York: Norton.

Griswold, Charles L., Jr. (1999). *Adam Smith and the Virtues of Enlightenment*, Cambridge: Cambridge University Press.

Grossbard-Shechtman, Shoshana, and Christopher Clague, eds. (2002). *The Expansion of Economics: Toward a More Inclusive Social Science*, Armonk, NY: M. E. Sharpe.

Halteman, James (1995). *The Clashing Worlds of Economics and Faith*. Scottdale, PA: Herald Press.

Halteman, James (2003). "Is Adam Smith's Moral Philosophy an Adequate Foundation for the Market Economy?" *Journal of Markets and Morality* 6:453–478.

Halteman, James (1999). "The Market System, The Poor and Economic Theory." In *Toward a Just and Caring Society*, David Gushee, ed. Grand Rapids, MI: Baker Books.

Hanley, Rayan Patrick (2009). *Adam Smith and the Character of Virtue*. Cambridge: Cambridge University Press.

Hayek, Friedrich (1937). "Economics and Knowledge." *Economica* 4:33–54.

Hayek, Friedrich (1955). *Science and Freedom*. London: Martin Secker and Warburg.

Hayek, Friedrich (1972 [1944]). *The Road to Serfdom*. Chicago: University of Chicago Press.

Hayek, Friedrich (1976). *Law, Legislation and Liberty*. Vol. 2, *The Mirage of Social Justice*. Chicago: University of Chicago Press.

Hayek, Friedrich (1983a). "Competition as a Discovery Procedure." In *The Essence of Hayek*, Chiaki Nishiyama and Kurt R. Leube, eds. Stanford, CA: Hoover Institution Press.

Hayek, Friedrich (1983b). "The Use of Knowledge in Society." In *The Essence of Hayek*, Chiaki Nishiyama and Kurt R. Leube, eds. Stanford, CA: Hoover Institution Press.

Hayek, Friedrich (1983c). "Two Pages of Fiction: The Impossibility of Socialist Calculation." In *The Essence of Hayek*, Chiaki Nishiyama and Kurt R. Leube, eds. Stanford, CA: Hoover Institution Press.

Hirschleifer, Jack (1985). "Expanding the Domain of Economics." *American Economic Review* 75:53–68.

Hirschman, Albert O. (1977). *The Passions and the Interests: Political Arguments for Capitalism before Its Triumph.* Princeton, NJ: Princeton University Press.

Hodgson, Geoffrey M. (2005). "The Present Position of Economics" by Alfred Marshall, *Journal of Institutional Economics* 1:121–137.

Houser D., and K. McCabe (2009) "Experimental Neuroeconomics and Non-cooperative Games." In *Neuroeconomics: Decision Making and the Brain,* P. Glimcher, C. Camerer, E. Fehr, and R. Poldrack, eds. Amsterdam: Academic Press.

Iannaccone, Lawrence R. (1994). "Why Strict Churches Are Strong." *American Journal of Sociology* 99: 1180–1211.

Jevons, William Stanley (1954 [1888]). *Theory of Political Economy.* In *Source Readings in Economic Thought,* P. Newman, A. D. Gayer, and M. H. Spencer, eds. New York: Norton.

Kaplan, H., and M. Gurven (2005). "A Natural History of Human Food Sharing and Cooperation: A Review and a New Multi-Individual Approach to the Negotiation of Norms." In *Moral Sentiments and Material Interests,* H. Gintis, S. Bowles, R. Boyd, and E. Fehr, eds. Cambridge: MA, MIT Press.

Katz, Leo (1996). *Ill-Gotten Gains: Evasion, Blackmail, Fraud, and Kindred Puzzles of the Law.* Chicago: University of Chicago Press.

Kaye, Joel. (1998). "Monetary and Market Consciousness in Thirteenth and Fourteenth Century Europe." In *Ancient and Medieval Economic Ideas and Concepts of Social Justice,* S. T. Lowry and B. Gordon, eds. Leiden, The Netherlands: E. J. Brill.

Keynes, John Maynard (2003 [1932]). *Essays in Persuasion* (orig. publ. New York, Brace). In *The History of Economic Thought: A Reader,* Steven G. Medema and Warren J. Samuels, eds. London: Routledge.

Keynes, John Maynard (1937). "The General Theory of Unemployment." *Quarterly Journal of Economics* 2: 209–223.

Keynes, John Maynard (1965 [1936]). *The General Theory of Employment, Interest and Money.* New York: Harcourt Brace and World.

Kirman, Alan (1999). "The Future of Economic Theory." In *Economics beyond the Millennium,* Alan Kirman and Louis-Andre Gerard-Varet, eds. Oxford: Oxford University Press.

Kirman, Alan, and Louis-Andre Gerard-Varet, eds. (1999). *Economics beyond the Millennium.* Oxford: Oxford University Press.

Klamer, Arjo (2007). *Speaking of Economics: How to Get in the Conversation.* London: Routledge.

Kleer, Richard A. (1993). "Adam Smith on the Morality of the Pursuit of Fortune." *Journal of Economics and Philosophy* 2: 289–295.

Klein, Peter J. (1992). "Introduction." In *The Fortunes of Liberalism: Essays on Austrian Economics and the Ideal of Freedom. The Collected Works of F. A. Hayek,* Indianapolis: Liberty Fund.

Koford, Kenneth J., and Jeffrey B. Miller (1991). "Habit, Custom, and Norms in Economics." In *Social Norms and Economic Institutions,* Kenneth J. Koford and Jeffrey B. Miller, eds. Ann Arbor: University of Michigan Press.

Langholm, Odd (1982). "Economic Freedom and the Scholastics." *History of Political Economy* 14: 260–283.

Langholm, Odd (1992). *Economics in the Medieval Schools: Wealth, Exchange, Value, Money, and Usury According to the Paris Theological Tradition 1200–1350.* Leiden, The Netherlands: E.J. Brill.

Langholm, Odd (1998a). *The Legacy of Scholasticism in Economic Thought: Antecedents of Choice and Power.* Cambridge: Cambridge University Press.

Langholm, Odd (1998b). "The Medieval Schoolmen 1200–1400." in *Economic Ideas and Concepts of Social Justice,* 439–502. S.Todd Lowry and Barry Gordon, eds. Leiden, The Netherlands: E.J. Brill.

Langholm, Odd (2003). *The Merchant in the Confessional: Trade and Price in the Pre-Reformation Penitential Handbooks.* Leiden, The Netherlands: E. J. Brill.

Leathers, Charles G. (1990). "Veblen and Hayek on Instincts and Evolution." *Journal of the History of Economic Thought* 12:162–178.

Leibenstein, Harvey (1950) "Bandwagon, Snob, and Veblen Effects in the Theory of Consumer Demand." In *Readings in Microeconomics,* W. Breit and H. M. Hochman, eds. 2nd ed. New York: Holt, Rinehart and Winston.

Lekachman, Robert. (1967). Introduction to Thorstein Veblen's *Absentee Ownership: The Case of America.* Boston: Beacon Press.

Leube, Kurt R. (1983). "Friedrich August von Hayek: A Biographical Introduction." In *The Essence of Hayek.* Chiaki Nishiyama and Kurt R. Leube, eds. Stanford, CA: Hoover Institution Press.

MacIntyre, Alasdair (1984). *After Virtue.* 2nd ed. Notre Dame: University of Notre Dame Press.

Mackie, Christopher D. (1998). *Canonizing Economic Theory: How Theories and Ideas Are Selected in Economics.* Armonk, NY: M. E. Sharpe.

Malthus, Thomas Robert (1976 [1798]). *An Essay on the Principle of Population.* Ed. Philip Appleman. New York: Norton.

Marshall, Alfred (1920 [1890]). *Principles of Economics,* 8th ed. London: Macmillan.

Marshall, Alfred (1925 [1885]). "The Present Position of Economics." In *Memorials of Alfred Marshall,* A. C. Pigou, ed. London: Macmillan, 152–174.

Marx, Karl, and F. Engels. (1971 [1848]). *The Communist Manifesto TCM.* In *Birth of the Communist Manifesto,* Dirk J. Struik, ed. New York: International Publishers.

Marx, Karl (1964). *Early Writings*. [EW]. Trans. and ed. T. B. Bottomore. New York: McGraw-Hill.

Marx, Karl (1976). *The German Ideology*. in Vol.5, *Karl Marx and Frederick Engels Collected Works*. [CW]. New York: International Publishers.

Marx, Karl (1977 [1861]). *Capital: A Critique of Political Economy*. Vol. 1. Trans. Ben Fowles. New York: Vintage Books.

Maslow, A. H., (1943). "A Theory of Human Motivation," Originally published in the *Psychological Review* 50, 370–396. Available at an internet resource developed by Christopher D. Green, "Classics in the History of Psychology," Toronto.

McCloskey, Dierdre N. (1998). *The Rhetoric of Economics*. 2nd ed. Madison: University of Wisconsin Press.

McCloskey, Deirdre N. (2006). *The Bourgeois Virtues*. Chicago: University of Chicago Press.

McGovern, John F. (1970). "The Rise of New Economic Attitudes—Economic Humanism, Economic Nationalism—during the Later Middle Ages and the Renaissance, A.D. 1200–1550." *Traditio* 26: 217–253.

Medema, Steven G., and Warren J. Samuels (2003). *The History of Economic Thought: A Reader*. London: Routledge.

Mendel, Arthur P. (1961). *Essential Works of Marxism*, USA: Bantom Books.

Mews, C. J., and I. Abraham (2007). "Usury and Just Compensation: Religious and Financial Ethics in Historical Perspective." *Journal of Business Ethics* 72:4.

Mill, John Stuart (1909 [1848]). *Principles of Political Economy* 7th ed. Ed. William J. Ashley, London: Longmans, Green.

Mises, Ludwig Von (1981 [1922]). *Socialism*. Trans. J. Kahane. Indianapolis: Liberty Classics.

Mokyr, Joel (2009). *The Enlightened Economy: An Economic History of Britain 1700–1850*.

New Haven, CT: Yale University Press.

Moulin, Hervé (1995). *Cooperative Microeconomics*, Princeton, NJ: Princeton University Press.

Moyle, J. B. (1967). *The Institutes of Justinian*. 5th ed. Trans. J. B. Moyle. Oxford: Oxford University Press.

Nelson, B. T. (1969 [1949]). *The Idea of Usury: From Tribal Brotherhood to Universal Otherhood*. 2nd ed. Chicago: University of Chicago.

Newman, P., A. D. Gayer, and M. H. Spencer (1954). *Source Readings in Economic Thought*, New York: Norton.

Noell, Edd S. (1995). "Adam Smith on Economic Justice in the Labor Market." *Journal of the History of Economic Thought* 17: 228–246.

Noell, Edd S. (1998). "Bargaining, Consent and the Just Wage in the Sources of Scholastic Economic Thought." *Journal of the History of Economic Thought* 20: 467–478.

Noell, Edd S. (2001). "In Pursuit of the Just Wage: A Comparison of Reformation and Counter-Reformation Economic Thought." *Journal of the History of Economic Thought* 23: 467–489.

Noell, Edd S. (2006). "Smith and a Living Wage: Competition, Economic Compulsion, and the Scholastic Legacy." *History of Political Economy* 38: 151–174.

Noell, Edd S. (2007a). "A 'Marketless World'? An Examination of Wealth and Exchange in the Gospels and First-Century Palestine." *Journal of Markets and Morality* 10: 85–114.

Noell, Edd S. (2007b). "Exchange and Property Rights in the Light of Biblical Values." *Journal of Private Enterprise* 22: 71–94.

North, Douglas C. (2005). *Understanding the Process of Economic Change.* Princeton, NJ: Princeton University Press.

O'Brien, D. P. (2004). *The Classical Economists Revisited.* Princeton, NJ: Princeton University Press.

Otteson, James (2002). *Adam Smith's Marketplace of Life.* Cambridge: Cambridge University Press.

Pareto, Vilfredo (1954 [1906]). *Manuel of Political Economy.* In *Source Readings in Economic Thought*, P. Newman, A. D. Gayer, and M. H. Spencer, eds. New York: Norton.

Parker, Philip M. (2000). *Physioeconomics: The Basis for Long Run Economic Growth.* Cambridge, MA: MIT Press.

Phillipson, Nicholas (2010). *Adam Smith: An Enlightened Life.* New Haven, CT: Yale University Press.

Pigou, A. C., ed. (1925). *Memorials of Alfred Marshall.* London: Macmillan.

Pinker, S. (1997). *How the Mind Works.* New York: Norton..

Plato (1961). *The Republic.* Trans. B. Jowett. New York: Vintage Books.

Posner, Richard A. (1983). *The Economics of Justice.* USA: President and Fellows of Harvard College.

Prychitko, David L. (1998). *Why Economists Disagree*, Albany: State University of New York Press.

Putnam, Hillary (2002). *The Collapse of the Fact/Value Dichotomy and Other Essays.* Cambridge, MA: Harvard University Press.

Rabin, Mathew (1998). "Psychology and Economics." *Journal of Economic Literature* 36:11–46.

Rand, Ayn (1993). *The Fountainhead.* New York: Penguin.

Raphael, D. D. (2007). *The Impartial Spectator: Adam Smith's Moral Philosophy.* Oxford: Oxford University Press.

Ricardo, David (1963). *The Principles of Political Economy and Taxation.* Homewood, IL: Richard D. Irwin.

Rima, Ingrid H. (1970). *Readings in the History of Economic Theory.* New York: Holt, Rinehardt and Winston.

Roncaglia, Alessandro. (2005). *The Wealth of Ideas: A History of Economic Thought.* Cambridge: Cambridge University Press.

Ross, Don (2005) *Economic Theory and Cognitive Science: Microexplanation.* Cambridge, MA: MIT Press.

Roth, Timothy (1999). *Ethics, Economics and Freedom.* Brookfield, VT: Ashgate.

Rutherford, Malcolm (1994). *Institutions in Economics.* Cambridge, UK: Cambridge University Press.

Say, J. B. (1824). *A Treatise on Political Economy.* Trans. C. R. Princep. Boston. Reprinted in Steven G. Medema and Warren J. Samuels, eds. (2003). *The History of Economic Thought: A Reader.* London: Routledge.

Schabas, Margaret (2005). *The Natural Origins of Economics.* Chicago: University of Chicago Press.

Schaefer, Kurt C., and Edd S. Noell (2005). "Contract Theory, Distributive Justice, and the Hebrew Sabbatical." *Faith and Economics* 45:1–19.

Schweiker, William, and Charles Mathewes, eds. (2004). *Having: Property and Possession in Religious and Social Life,* Grand Rapids, MI: Wm. B. Eerdmans.

Sen, Amartya. (1982). *Poverty and Famines: An Essay on Entitlement and Deprivation.* Oxford: Oxford University Press.

Sen, Amartya. (1988). *On Ethics and Economics.* Malden, MS: Blackwell.

Sent, Esther Mirjam (2004). "Behavioral Economics: How Psychology Made Its (Limited) Way Back into Economics." *History of Political Economy* 36:735–760.

Silk, Joan B. (2005). "The Evolution of Cooperation in Primate Groups." In *Moral Sentiments and Material Interests,* H. Gintis, S. Bowles, R. Boyd, and E. Fehr, eds., Cambridge, MA: MIT Press.

Smith, Adam (1976 [1759]). *The Theory of Moral Sentiments.* D. D. Raphael and A. L. Macfie, eds., Oxford: Oxford University Press.

Smith, Adam (1976 [1776]). *An Inquiry into the Nature and Causes of the Wealth of Nations.* Ed. R. H. Campbell and A. S. Skinner. Oxford: Clarendon Press.

Smith, Adam (1978 [1766]). *Lectures on Jurisprudence.* Ed. R. L.Meek, D. D Raphael, and P. G. Stein. Oxford: Oxford University Press.

Smith, Vernon L. (2008). *Rationality in Economics,* Cambridge, UK: Cambridge University Press.

Spiegel, Henry W. (1991). *The Growth of Economic Thought.* 3rd ed. Durham, NC: Duke University Press.

Struik, Dirk J. (1971). "Birth of the Communist Manifesto and Its Historical Significance." In *Birth of the Communist Manifesto,* Dirk. J. Struik, ed. New York: International Publishers.

Sunstein, Cass R. (2000). *Behavioral Law and Economics.* Cambridge, UK: Cambridge Cambridge University Press.

Tabb, William K. (1999). *Reconstructing Political Economy: The Great Divide in Economic Thought.* London: Routledge.

Tullock, Gordon (2005). *Public Goods, Redistribution and Rent Seeking.* Cheltenham, UK: Edward Elgar.

Tversky, Amos, and Daniel Kahneman (1981). "The Framing of Decisions and the Psychology of Choice." *Science* 211, 453–458.

Van Staveren, Irene (2001). *The Values of Economics: An Aristotelian Perspective.* London: Routledge.

Veblen, Thorstein (1898). "Why Economics Is Not an Evolutionary Science." *Quarterly Journal of Economics* 12:373–426.

Veblen, Thorstein (1963 [1921]). *The Engineers and the Price System.* New York: Harcourt, Brace, and World.

Veblen, Thorstein (1983 [1899]). *The Theory of the Leisure Class: An Economic Study of Institutions.* London: Unwin.

Veblen, Thorstein (2007 [1904]). *The Theory of Business Enterprise.* New York: Cosimo Classics.

Verburg, Rudi (2006). "John Stuart Mill's Political Economy: Educational Means to Moral Progress." *Review of Social Economy* 64:225–246.

Walras, Leon (1972). *Elements of Pure Economics.* Trans. William Jaffe. In Everett J. Burtt Jr., *Social Perspectives in the History of Economic Theory.* New York: St. Martins Press.

Werhane, Patricia (1991). *Adam Smith and His Legacy for Modern Capitalism.* New York: Oxford University Press.

Whalen, Charles J. (1996). "The Institutional Approach to Political Economy." In *Beyond Neoclassical Economics,* Fred Foldvary, ed. Cheltenham, UK: Edward Elgar.

Williamson, Oliver E. (1985). *The Economic Institutions of Capitalism.* New York: Free Press.

Williamson, Oliver E., and Sidney G. Winter, eds. (1993). *The Nature of the Firm: Origins, Evolution, and Development.* New York: Oxford Univeristy Press.

Winch, Peter, (1990). *The Idea of a Social Science and Its Relation to Philosophy.* 2nd ed. London: Routledge.

Young, Jeffery T. (1997). *Economics as a Moral Science: The Political Economy of Adam Smith.* Cheltenham, UK: Edward Elgar.

Young, Jeffrey T., ed. (2009). *Elgar Companion to Adam Smith.* Cheltenham, UK: Edward Elgar.

Zak, Paul J., ed. (2008). *Moral Markets: The Critical Role of Markets in the Economy.* Princeton, NJ: Princeton University Press.

Zey, Mary (1998). *Rational Choice Theory and Organizational Theory: A Critique.* Thousand Oaks, CA: Sage.

INDEX

competition and economic life as
    processes, 91
conflicted about religion, 58
dialogue with Stoic positions on moral
    life, 33, 70, 71, 74
fresh view of social organization, 143–144
moral philosophy, 62–84
moral reflection in his work, 58, 70, 75,
    83, 84, 91, 92
on deceit in the marketplace, 83, 86–89
on exchange, 80–82, 85
on human nature, 4, 187
on justice, 9–10, 56, 74, 75, 76, 80, 88
on malevolence, 83
on probity, 82, 86
on prudence, 56, 75, 79–80
on selfish passions, 62–63, 66, 75, 76,
    78, 83
on social passions, 61–62, 75, 78, 189
on sympathy, 60–66, 68, 71, 78, 85, 91,
    194, 195
on the all-seeing judge, 73–75, 80
on the division of labor, 81
on the human goal of self-preservation,
    59–60
on the impartial spectator, 63, 66–73,
    75, 78, 80, 82, 85, 86, 91, 194, 195
on the invisible hand, 75
on the moral foundations of commercial
    society, 81–82
on the unsocial passions, 75, 76, 78–79,
    85, 189
on vices of commercial society, 83
on virtue, 75
reading WN within the context of
    Smith's moral theory, 90–91
Scottish Enlightenment philosopher, 51
tensions in Smith's time, 55–56
snob appeal, 160
Social Darwinists on competition and
    beneficent order, 117
social norms, 160
sociopolitical economy, 182–189
Socrates, 27
Stoicism, 32
    form of natural theology relied upon by
        Smith, 58

major philosophical contributors, 32
moral reflection, 33
natural system, 33, 74
self control, 72
subprime mortgage lending, 52–53
    predatory practices, 53
    role in the financial crisis
        of 2008–2009, 52

Tabb, William K., 130, 150
technology changes medieval world,
    47, 55
telos, 16, 17, 23, 24, 26, 27, 28, 32, 54, 58,
    59, 68, 72, 84, 92, 114, 168, 169
    equation by Marx with human
        autonomy, 114
    Smith's concept, 74
theory of second best, 192
Thomas of Chobham, on debtors who pay
    usury voluntarily, 43–44
tit-for-tat strategy of game theory, 169
transaction costs, 149, 164
trust in economic relationships,
    170–172
    role in the financial crisis
        of 2008–2009, 171
Tullock, Gordon, 149
Tversky, Amos, 161–162

United Nations, 186
    Development Program human
        development index, 179
United States Constitution, 55
unsocial passions, 78
utility function and optimization, 34–35,
    131, 152, 157, 192

Veblen, Thorstein, 10, 108, 115, 121, 154,
    188, 195, 196
    critique of neoclassical marginalism
        and its conception of human nature,
        116–117
    critique of the price system, 120
    nonteleological orientation of his
        analysis, 120
    on a "soviet of technicians," 120
    on absentee owners of firms, 119–120